that side of heaven

Walking the Journey of Loss, Grief, and Healing after Miscarriage

BY HEATHER BUTLER

That Side of Heaven
By Heather Butler
Published by Faithfulness Declared
Colorado Springs, CO

Cover design by Lauren Stewart, www.stewartstudio.co

ISBN: 978-0-9995991-0-5

LCCN: 2017917322

Table of Contents

Acknowledgments

Lavender and Pine, I carry you both inside me with every breath I take. Jesus is using your lives to give light to the darkness, hope to the hopeless. Momma can't wait to embrace you both one day. We've got some catching up to do, my darlings.

Jarred, you are my best friend and my most wild adventure. Thank you for carrying me through this journey and supporting my heart as I step into my sacred calling.

Momma and Meagan, you are my precious gifts. A cord of three strands is not easily broken.

Aunt Anna, your open hands and heart showed me the hands and heart of Jesus. I am forever grateful for and changed by your faithfulness.

Our Harling family, you love us so well. Thank you for doing life with us.

Introduction

Oh, precious friend, I am so sorry for the loss you're experiencing. My heart is wrapped around yours, and my tears flow with yours. Please know you are *not* alone.

My passionate prayer is that through the words and stories within these pages you find community—a circle of mommas who understand what you're going through. There is rawness here. There is vulnerability and honesty . . . and some of it is ugly. But every word is shared with you in mind—you precious momma, whose heart is broken. I want you to know that your pain, anger, confusion, and sadness are valid. As impossible as it may feel right now, I also want you to know that there is hope and healing to come.

We lose so much after miscarriage. We lose the little lives that were a part of our very own bodies. We lose the babies that we should have held and watched grow up. We lose the future children that we envisioned. We mourn the dreams and hopes that will never come to be. We helplessly watch as the plans we had for our growing families crumble away. We have no control over any of it, and that can bring brokenness, anger, confusion.

Perhaps you lost your baby the same day that you found out you were pregnant. Or maybe you carried your baby for months—even feeling little wiggles and kicks. No matter what the details of your story are or how far along you were, your baby has changed you and is forever a part of your story. Every emotion and every pain is very real, and just as every baby is unique, so is each mother's grief.

There is no clear outline as to what your journey will look like, nor is there a precise time line of healing to which your heart will adhere. Your journey is distinct. Your time frame follows the pace of your heart, not the other way around. It may not happen today. It may not happen tomorrow. But I promise you, if you allow Jesus into your rawness, he will comfort you and bring a wholeness to your heart like only he can.

It is not just the details of my own story that I tenderly hand to you; there are parts of other stories here—stories from five other loss-mommas who want to share their journeys of loss and of hope with you. But more than anything, this book is meant to be *yours*. Your story is woven into to each word. Own the truth that is proclaimed. It is for *you*. At the end of each chapter you will find a section that includes God's Promise, A Prayer, and a Journal prompt. Use these sections to absorb, process, and express what is going on inside of your own heart.

My hope is that this book becomes a companion to you as you begin to navigate through this unfamiliar, messy territory. I hope to be a friend who whispers God's promises to you when you cannot utter them for yourself—and to remind you that God remains faithful.

The beautiful moment you conceived, your precious little one made you a momma for all eternity. You are a part of a sacred sisterhood—we are mommas on this side of heaven loving and celebrating the lives of our babies on that side of heaven.

Love to you,
Heather

Meet the Mommas

Amy

Amy is a follower of Christ, wife, and mommy to two kids, two spoiled tabby cats, and a little one she is waiting to meet in heaven. When she's not chasing or posting adorable pictures of her kids on social media, she has the privilege of walking alongside others as a licensed professional counselor in Texas. Amy is a theology junkie, women's Bible study leader, wannabe chef, wordsmith, and champion Boggle player.

Anneke

Anneke lives in Virginia and is the wife of twelve years to her amazing husband. She has a very loud house, bursting at the seams with five lively children—one big-sister/book-reading/glitter-and-rainbow-wearing/gymnast girl, and then four little-brother/floor-wrestling/soccer-playing/inappropriate-noise-making/cuddle-master boys. She and her husband have four more children in heaven whom they greatly miss and are excited to meet someday.

Erin

Erin and her husband have been married for eleven years and live with their two sons in Missouri. Her husband's head is often in the clouds (literally) since he is a Black Hawk helicopter pilot for the army. Their older son is the typical oldest child. He loves Jesus, is so kind, and challenges Erin daily in her middle school math skills. He is already better at math than she is (but thankfully doesn't know it yet). Their younger son joined their family through the miracle of adoption; he is brave, sweet, and always wanting to help others. Everything in her family's life is because of Jesus and his unending love. They have endured great trauma, and it is only because of Jesus that they are able to choose joy. Erin feels humbled and honored to walk this earth telling others about all the things God has done in her life.

Keri

Keri currently lives in California with her husband, who is an officer in the navy. They have a son and baby daughter. Keri is a worship leader, and her connection to God through music has been vital in her grieving and healing journey. She has learned that regardless of outcome and circumstances, God is still worthy to be praised.

Megan

Megan and her husband live in sunny California. She is a full-time homemaker and professional baby wrangler to their three beautiful daughters. She also has a daughter named Eliana waiting for them in heaven. Megan has known God's faithfulness throughout her life. Even after Eliana's death, when she cried out in pain and hurt, asking the whys, she felt God's presence and believes that God is true to his word that "he will never leave you nor forsake you" (Deut. 31:6 NIV).

CHAPTER ONE

broken

There is a unique pain that
comes from preparing your heart
for a child that never comes.
—David Platt

My life-altering journey began on the morning of October 1, 2011, when I was thirteen weeks and one day pregnant. It was a Saturday, so my husband, Jarred, was home with me. Before we made breakfast or sat together to drink our coffee, I went to the restroom. And I saw what every pregnant woman dreads—blood. My heart dropped and my hands began to tremble. It took a moment for my brain to process what my eyes were seeing. It wasn't a lot of blood, and I had spotted very lightly a couple times during the earliest weeks of this pregnancy, so my mind immediately tried to convince my heart that this was nothing different—even though there was more blood than the previous times. I wasn't in any pain, so I stayed hopeful. Something like a miscarriage wouldn't . . . couldn't . . . happen to *me*. I was young. I was healthy. I was going to have a normal pregnancy and a healthy baby. That's what was going to happen. A miscarriage was one of those rare things that happened to other women. I thought.

Jarred and I had prayed for this child before we even knew I was pregnant. Every morning before Jarred left for work, he would lay his hand on my stomach and pray for our baby—for perfect health and development and protection. We knew God was faithful. We had experienced his faithfulness many times in our lives. We had seen him provide for us in ways that were completely unexpected, completely miraculous. We believed. We knew. We had seen. But now our prayers had shifted away from ourselves, and we began crying out to God to spare our baby. Our need for him was intertwined with fear and deep desperation. I never knew a heart could hold so many emotions at once.

I called my midwife, desperately wanting her to tell me it was going to be okay, that this was totally normal. I wanted her to tell me that blood could mean something else—something unrelated to the life of my baby. But as she began talking to me, the hope I was trying to stay attached to felt like it was dangling by a thread. The sound in her voice, and how she was preparing me for what I may see and experience, shook my entire world. Since I was thirteen weeks along, she warned that I might see a more formed baby if everything were to come out naturally.

This can't be happening. This can't be happening.

The following hours were painfully slow. The cramps intensified, and my body began to push out more than just blood. The waves of pain began to wash over me. I now know that pain as a contraction. I was in labor. I would sit in the bathroom with my husband and let the pain subside and then go back and sit on the couch. I would pray that the bleeding would suddenly stop—that our fear would turn to victory and that the life of our baby would be that of a miracle. With every trip to the bathroom, I had to prepare myself for what I might see. Finally, I began to hear substance splash in the toilet water. And every time I would wonder, *Was that my baby?* I began passing things that should have continued to grow and stay in my body for six more months. I couldn't believe it.

The thing that couldn't happen to me *was* happening.

I hadn't passed anything that resembled a little baby, but the realization started to sink in for both of us. My precious husband told me not to look at anything and that he would take care of it. He collected every piece that was being stolen from my body and placed it in a container of water. We wanted to save it all to ensure we had our baby. Oh, how his heart was hurting too. He had no control over what was happening and was just trying to do whatever he could to comfort me.

By early evening the blood was heavy, but there was still no baby. The pain no longer came in waves—it was now constant and had deepened and strengthened exponentially.

I felt as if my insides were being torn apart. We decided to go to the hospital, if anything for pain control. My uncle and aunt who lived nearby drove us to the ER. What was only a fifteen-minute drive felt so much longer. When we arrived, I could barely stand. I could barely think or breathe normally. I had never experienced such physical pain. It overshadowed any emotions I was feeling. I truly felt I was dying, and it terrified me. I spoke Jesus's name over and over and over again, begging for rescue and relief. I faded in and out of reality. Multiple times I began blacking out because my body just couldn't endure the relentless pain any longer.

As I lay shaking on the hospital bed, I writhed in agony and continuously repositioned myself, desperately searching for an ounce of relief. But there was none. The nurse repeatedly tried to insert an IV in my right arm. Finally, she moved to my left arm and was able to. I told the doctor it wasn't going to be much longer before I passed out. I figured that was a good piece of information he should have. I had hit a physical and mental wall that was just too dense to push through. I knew it was a matter of minutes before I lost consciousness. Jarred stood helplessly by my side. He found a nurse to get me a warm blanket. He held my hand. He prayed for me aloud. That's all he could do. He stood as my rock during the scariest time of our lives.

After forty-five minutes of what felt like a nonstop contraction, the doctor put something in my IV and the excruciating pain finally began to lessen. I didn't care what he had given me or how much. I just wanted it to keep coming. I have never been so thankful for pain relief. But as the physical pain subsided, I became more mentally present and aware—and then the emotional pain exploded. I remember the doctor's words as he began examining me. "Yeah, I don't like this. I see tissue." *Tissue*. Tissue that formed my baby's body. As Jarred held my hand, he began reminding me, "Our God remains faithful. No matter what happens. He is faithful."

He is faithful. He is faithful. He is faithful . . .

During the entire previous year, the Lord had been pressing that very truth upon our hearts—that despite how our emotions and circumstances change, he would always remain faithful to us. And now, in a white-walled hospital room, we were clinging to that promise. Our heads knew it before. But now we had the opportunity to walk in it. Purposely and intentionally, to take one step of faith at a time and begin walking down this broken, jagged road. Jarred gently asked me over and over, "Do you believe he is faithful to you?"

"I know he is faithful. I believe he is faithful," I answered again and again. I saw the nurses' curious glances at my husband as he kept speaking God's promises and truth over me when instead he could have been cursing at God, justifiably angry. As real as the physical and emotional pain was, the Holy Spirit's presence was almost tangible in that emergency room. Every breath held both pain and peace. It was in that exact moment that the peace that defies all human logic, which God's Word talks about, truly became real to me.

And the peace of God, which surpasses all understanding, will guard your hearts and your minds in Christ Jesus.
Philippians 4:7 (ESV)

Jarred watched as a gush of blood poured into the container that the doctor was holding. He sent it to the lab and told a nurse to take us upstairs for an ultrasound to confirm everything was out. Even then, I held onto frayed hope that a heartbeat would be found. I still wanted a miracle. The nurse began pushing my gurney upstairs to the ultrasound room as Jarred walked beside me. I watched the lights on the ceiling pass one by one like a tragic scene in a dramatic movie. The moment was surreal and filled me with so many thoughts that it left me numb. All I could do was lie there. Lie there and try to piece together what was happening.

The ultrasound technician was soft-spoken with a gentle demeanor. She looked at me tenderly. Without saying a word, she expressed so much. The room was dark and peaceful, a welcome change of scenery. It felt completely detached from the brightly lit, lively, and crowded floor below, becoming an odd kind of sanctuary of sorts. Jarred interlaced his fingers with mine while the ultrasound technician remained focus on the objective: to take internal images to see if my uterus was empty.

She placed her right hand on the computer keys and stared at the large screen in front of her. Click. She took the first picture. Click. Click. I held my breath and watched her face for any sort of hopeful expression or positive signal. But there was none.

Click. *Please God, please let her find something.*

Click. *Please find a heartbeat. Jesus, let there be a heartbeat.*

After a few minutes of silence, we asked if there was a heartbeat. She compassionately responded, "I'm sorry. I don't see a heartbeat . . . or anything else."

That was the final confirmation. My womb was empty and so was my heart. The emptiness didn't feel hollow, though; it felt so very heavy. The void was deep. Our baby was gone. The pain I had endured was labor, but I would not be bringing my baby home. Such a cruel realization. What should have been the beginning of a life had become the end. Jarred spoke the Lord's truth over me once again, then walked out to the hallway to call our families. I could hear him crying. He could barely get the words out. "We lost the baby." My heart shattered.

The nurse brought me back down to my room. Shortly after, a chaplain came in. There was a comforting strength about him. His compassionate countenance was covered by a thick salt-and-pepper beard. I'm sure he had opened many hospital doors where hurting families were waiting on the other side. I'm sure he had talked with other couples who had lost their babies. I'm sure he had willingly entered into the heartbreak of countless other souls before us. But in those moments with us, he was fully present. The words he spoke and the sympathy he showed were authentic, and his care was genuine. I asked him if the doctors were sure that the baby was in that gush of blood that the doctor sent to the lab. He left the room for a few minutes to verify, then came back in and told us that the baby had indeed come out in that moment. I was thankful that we didn't have to experience that part at home. A substantial amount of bloody matter had continuously left my body all day long, but the baby stayed inside of me until the doctor was there. For that, I was strangely grateful.

The chaplain brought me a long, mint-green shawl that was crocheted thanks to a ministry at the hospital. He carefully laid it down the length of my body and told me its purpose was to comfort a grieving mother, even in a small way. I wiggled my fingers in between the soft, lush yarn as he went over the options of final arrangements for our baby. We decided to have our baby cremated. The ashes would be spread near a memorial bench where other babies' ashes had also been freed. It brought me comfort to know that if I couldn't hold my baby, at least my baby's body would be with other precious little ones.

In the middle of the night, I was released from the hospital. As I began to get dressed, I realized there was blood on everything. It was overwhelming and frustrating. I just wanted to go home—home to my own shower, my own sheets, my own walls. Jarred grabbed countless paper towels and helped me clean up enough to leave. My uncle and aunt who had stayed in the waiting room the entire time then drove us to a grocery store to pick up the things we would need over the next few days. Because I had been pregnant and didn't have a period, I didn't have pads or supplies at home for the bleeding that would continue. My uncle and husband went inside, and my aunt waited in the car with me. I looked out the car window and watched my husband as he walked inside. I noticed how silent and still everything was, like the entire world was frozen.

The words my aunt offered in those painful, quiet morning hours will forever stay with me. She had also lost a baby and shared her story. She opened that tender part of her heart and allowed me in. I saw her grief even though her loss had happened many years before. I saw her pain, but she also gave me a glimpse of hope. Hope for healing, hope for the future, hope for some form of normal again. She knew firsthand what I was going through. Her feet had once stood on the terrain that I was now navigating through. She understood the physical pain. She understood the heartache of not bringing home a baby after a pregnancy. She understood it all. And that brought my heart a little comfort. As my aunt offered words of life to me while we sat in the car, my uncle was doing the same for Jarred as they were in the grocery store. "You are still a father," he told Jarred.

These were words that we both held on to for many months to come. We were still parents. I was still a mommy.

That baby forever made me a mother and nothing could change that.

As we settled in for the night, the rooms of our condo didn't offer the familiarity I had looked forward to. It felt like I had been gone for months. Have you ever had that feeling? Leaving your home for an extended amount of time and then coming back to it? You recognize it, you know it, but it feels so unfamiliar.

Everything felt different. But more than anything, I felt different. I was changed. And I knew I would never ever be the same person I was. My husband and I sat together. We were both completely drained. The only other thing left to do was go to bed, but it felt strange for some reason. Maybe because going to sleep is a normal part of a day, but this day had become a life-altering one. There was nothing normal about it, so anything routine felt out of place.

Getting to sleep was nearly impossible, both physically and emotionally. Once I did fall asleep, it wasn't deep and it didn't last long. And every time I woke up, my heart drowned in deep and overwhelming sorrow. It wrenched in agony and my mournful wails echoed loudly through the night. My entire body cried. And the only thing I could do was lie there, wrapped in my husband's arms and my mint-green shawl, and cry.

The morning brought a new reality. A pain-filled reality. So many thoughts invaded my mind. The first thing I wanted to do was let our friends know. But I didn't want to interact or talk to anyone yet. I wasn't ready to relive it all or answer questions.

I didn't have anything to give, but I wanted them to know. So my husband texted friends and wrote on his social media informing everyone of what happened.

Immediately, an outpouring of kind words and support began to fill our inboxes and phones. But something surprised me. I began receiving story after story from friends who had also lost babies—some years ago, others more recently. Many of these women I had known for a very long time, yet I had no knowledge about this part of their lives—this part of their hearts.

I wasn't alone. It was nice to feel understood, but I knew my baby's life was unique. And my brokenness was my own.

Amy's Story

After trying for just under a year, I was thrilled when I found out I was pregnant! I knew I had missed my cycle, so we found out very early. I went and bought my husband a card to tell him when he got home from work. At around eight weeks we found out that miscarriage was likely, but, as I say, "I wanted to leave a little room for Jesus." I was hoping for a miracle. But we finally miscarried at twelve weeks. Physically it was tough, but from talking with other women who have suffered loss in this way I realized it was relatively mild—and fast. The emotional pain was far worse. I was out of town working when I started to bleed. My coworkers in ministry were precious, but I felt alone. My husband drove two hours to pick me up and drove me home in the pouring rain. All I could do was cry. I was up most of the night with cramping and bleeding, and around midnight it was over. After everything was over, I felt empty. I knew there had been life inside of me, and now it was gone. I also felt tremendous loss. The loss of our child would have been enough to grieve, but I also felt like I was grieving the hope of having a family. I knew we would likely get pregnant again, but it didn't matter. I wanted this baby.

Erin's Story

I was extremely excited when I found out I was pregnant with our second child! When we told our son that we were pregnant with his baby brother or sister, he was the most excit-ed almost-three-year-old you could find! To give him the gift of being a brother felt amazing. Our family was growing and we were beyond excited!

We brought our son with us to our first ultrasound to see our newest baby! We heard the baby's heartbeat, fast and strong, and I teared up at the miracle of this little life we created. I remember seeing that sweet little baby's hand wave across the screen and watching the backflips and wriggles. I could clearly see the outline of a precious baby on that black-and-white ultrasound screen. But just as quickly as I could see the outline of our baby, panic fiercely struck across the nurse's face. She quickly turned off the heartbeat monitor and flipped the screen out of our view. Fear washed over my husband and me as we looked back and forth at each other and the ultrasound nurse. She abruptly said, "I will be right back." She quickly returned with the doctor, and another nurse came in to get our son to entertain him while we talked to the doctor. The doctor scanned over the baby again, this time in complete silence as pain and confusion set in. As the doctor turned off the ultrasound screen, he began to explain to us that this wasn't a viable pregnancy and that our baby wouldn't survive—it was an ectopic pregnancy. Because this pregnancy was in my fallopian tube instead of my uterus, it could burst at any time. The baby would die as well as cause me to go into shock and bleed internally, putting my life at risk. He explained that because I was so far along, the methotrexate shot typically used for an ectopic pregnancy wouldn't work and that I would need to have emergency surgery within hours to save my life.

All I could think was, *How can this sweet little baby whose hand I just saw wave across the ultrasound screen not be a viable pregnancy?* I was in shock and denial.

Having just been told that our sweet little baby wouldn't survive, I was about to be rushed into emergency surgery to save my life, which I hadn't even known was threatened in the first place. It would take time that I didn't have to let that soak in. I refused to sign the consent form for hours. My sweet husband reminded me that we already had a baby at home who needed a mommy and that I needed to sign the papers so they could do surgery. It was the hardest thing I'd ever had to do. It's like I was signing away my rights to this baby and his or her life. I knew once I signed it that I was agreeing that my baby wouldn't survive. It went against every fiber of my being to sign that paper, but I did sign it. Very quickly after that, I was put to sleep and the surgery began.

I woke up to a whole new reality. That is a day I will never forget. I will never forget the look on my husband's face as his tear-filled eyes told me that our baby—which we found out was a girl—was gone. I was told that because of the emergency surgery, my ability to have any more children biologically in the future was gone as well. Everything was stripped away from me in that moment.

During surgery, they opened me all the way up. I call it my C-section scar because that's what it is. I did deliver a baby that day, even if the baby wasn't full-term and even though the baby didn't survive. Once the surgery began and I was opened up on the surgery table, the doctor said blood just poured out of me. It took him by surprise, and he said he originally thought that I was hemorrhaging because my fallopian tube had burst already. But in reality he found out that it was actually my right ovary that had hemorrhaged months prior and was bleeding.

My ovary had burst and I had no idea! I had been internally bleeding for months, which in effect may have caused my ectopic pregnancy. We ended up losing not only our baby but also my fallopian tube she was in and my ovary on the opposite side. My parts wouldn't ever again connect naturally to conceive another child. Our hearts were broken in that moment for a lifetime. That day we suffered the loss of our baby girl as well as our ability to have any more biological children.

Megan's Story

My daughter was seventeen months old when I took a pregnancy test and found out that she was going to be a big sister! We started telling family and friends a few weeks later, and everyone was just as thrilled as we were.

During the ultrasound at my first prenatal appointment at about ten weeks, we discovered there was fluid under our baby's skin in the abdomen, on the back, and around the skull. The doctor couldn't tell us exactly what it was without testing, but she did say it was most likely a chromosomal abnormality and that with the large amount of fluid present that early on, the chances of baby's survival was almost none. I couldn't accept the doctor's words and decided to get a second opinion at another hospital, but they said the same thing. I saw a genetic specialist to weigh my options for genetic testing, and we decided on the least invasive test called Cell-Free Fetal DNA (cffDNA). They told us the test could take one to two weeks to get the results back. They drew my blood, and then we waited. We took a mini vacation to the mountains to help distract us and also to begin praying and pleading for the life of the child inside of me.

A few days before my next ultrasound the genetic specialist called me back with the results—it was a sex-chromosome abnormality specifically called Turner's Syndrome (TS). Turner's Syndrome is only found in women—this is how we found out we had another daughter. TS is a sex-chromosomal disorder when the X chromosomes are fully or partially missing. There are women living with TS, but because of the higher level of fluid within my baby's body, they gave her a 5 percent chance of survival.

We went to our next ultrasound appointment at twelve weeks with positive attitudes and hope in our hearts. The nurse initially started off with just using a Doppler test and told us not to worry if she couldn't find the heartbeat because she was new. After she tried and couldn't find the heartbeat, she let the doctor know and they wheeled in the ultrasound machine. The second the baby came on the screen, I knew. Her little body lay at the bottom of the screen lifeless. My heart sank. The doctor began talking to me about what needed to happen next. It felt weird moving on so fast—as if this child wasn't a child but a disease that merely needed to be dispelled from my body as soon as possible. I chose not to have a D&C but to pass the baby naturally. They gave me a month for this to happen. The doctor told me a miscarriage would not be painful, but simply like menstrual cramps. She said I would bleed when I passed the fetus, so I needed to have pads on hand. And she gave me a cup to bring "the fetus" back in to do additional testing. I know she didn't mean it to be, but it felt heartless. She was a good doctor; she did her job. And in the moment, I was okay with just getting the details I needed so that I could get out of the hospital and be with my family. I don't exactly remember the rest of that day, just that I went to bed that night feeling empty. The next day was when the emotions hit hard. I had to move on with life and act as if nothing ever happened. My baby was still inside of me but not alive. And not too many people knew. Not the airlines I had to call to cancel an upcoming trip, not the bank teller, not the grocery store clerk, not even the neighbor who came by that day to say hi. It was so very difficult.

It was a long two weeks before I finally felt the pains of labor. The doctor had said cramps, but they were not just cramps. Thankfully I had reached out to a friend of mine who had also lost a baby right at around twelve weeks' gestation. She shared her experience with me and told me to expect real labor pains. I felt more prepared after talking to her, and thankfully I wasn't brutally surprised with labor pains when I would have expected only menstrual-like cramps.

So at fourteen weeks' gestation I lay awake in the middle of the night feeling my uterus contract over and over. It hurt, not as intense as full-term labor because my uterus was still so small, but it was enough to keep me awake all night. I got a couple hours of sleep before waking again around seven a.m. I rolled onto my side and knew that as soon as I stood up I would need to get to the bathroom quickly. I woke my husband up before I stood, and told him I needed him to help me once I got to the bathroom. I stood up, and as I quickly walked to the bathroom, I felt blood on my legs and then the rush of everything falling out of me right as I sat down on the toilet. My husband entered the bathroom in a panic, seeing there was blood everywhere. After sitting for a moment, I realized I needed to get my baby; I wasn't going to leave her in the toilet. I asked my husband to help me get her out so he reached in, searching for a little body. I started crying as soon as I saw her. My husband just held her in his hand. There she was, about half the size of the palm of his hand. We looked at her little arms and her little fingers, and the lids of her eyes. I was an emotional mess, and I didn't know what to do. I reached for the cup the doctor had given me, hesitant but numb, and I gently placed her in it.

Since I was bleeding so much and felt so light-headed, the doctor suggested we go to the emergency room. Once we were at the ER, everything seemed to slow down; there really wasn't much to do except sit and go through the motions. They checked to make sure I had passed everything, and they made sure I hadn't lost too much blood; that was about it. I felt an odd sense of relief that it was all over—it had been a long month of waiting. My only regret was that I just let them take my little girl, in a cup, only to be tested for reasons that didn't matter to me anymore. My heart breaks that I just let her go. I guess my excuse is, I was so numb to it all in that moment.

God's Promise

The LORD is near to the brokenhearted;
and saves the crushed in spirit.
Psalm 34:18 (ESV)

A Prayer

My God,

I don't understand why this has happened. I am broken, Father. I need you. I need your comfort and peace. I need your healing, both physically and emotionally. There are moments when I can barely breathe, much less lift my hands to you. So hold me, Jesus, and show me you are near. Enter into this brokenness with me. Anchor your truth so deep inside my heart that no matter how hard the violent waves of pain and doubt crash over me, I will remain standing firm on your promises. Hide me in your shelter. In Jesus's name, amen.

Journal

Whether you feel God's presence closely or he feels painfully distant, his Word says that he remains with you. He is not watching you from a distance as you mourn and grieve. He is a close God. An intimate God. A good God who remains as close to you as the breath in your lungs. He is pulling your tired body and weary heart near to him.

God's Word tells the story of Lazarus (John 11:1–44). Jesus loved Lazarus and his sisters, Mary and Martha. By the time Jesus arrived where Lazarus was, Lazarus had died. Mary told Jesus, "'Lord, if you had been here, my brother would not have died.' When Jesus saw her weeping, and the Jews who had come with her also weeping, he was deeply moved in his spirit and greatly troubled. And he said, 'Where have you laid him?' They said to him, 'Lord, come and see.' Jesus wept" (John 11:32–35 ESV). The Son of God, who understood eternal truths greater than anyone, wept. Jesus knew that physical death was not final, and he fully understood the glory of heaven. But he loved Lazarus and was moved by those who were mourning—and he wept.

Write a prayer conversation between you and God about your loss. Allow yourself to write honestly. He isn't shocked or offended by your pain, anger, or emptiness. He wants you to invite him into those raw places so he can show you his faithfulness and breathe healing into you.

CHAPTER TWO

branded

What we have once enjoyed
we can never lose. All that we love
deeply becomes a part of us.
—Helen Keller

The days felt abnormally long, but before I knew it, two weeks had gone by. As I began figuring out what my new normal looked like, I filled the hours with crocheting, drawing, and reading. I kept gravitating towards drawing pregnant silhouettes. The outline of a round stomach remained achingly beautiful to me—that fullness of life inside a womb—it was something I hadn't experienced to its greatest extent, yet mourned the loss of nonetheless.

At the first sign of a cramp, I would recoil in fear. Those deep contractions lingered for over a week—triggering an emotional reaction in me every single time. My body recognized the pain and would tense up, anticipating the cramps to intensify like they had before. Each day they slowly weakened in strength. And after a couple weeks of being on edge and dreading even the slightest twinge of discomfort, the cramps and bleeding had completely stopped.

Emotionally, I felt unpredictable. Without any warning I would break down—my heart responding to memories of losing my baby before my brain could catch up. The sobbing would catch me off guard, and I would have to stop whatever I was doing and just cry. My eyes would flood and overflow with tears of mourning. They were a different kind of tears—heavier and thicker. They came in such quantity that my surroundings looked as if I was under water. A fitting concept since I felt like I was drowning too. My fingers would tingle, and I would have to be intentional about catching my breath. Then after the wave of grief had washed over me, I would take a deep breath and try to keep doing life that day.

I worried about my baby's tiny body. The idea of my baby being alone somewhere—just lying there—made me sick to my stomach. Moments of panic would grip me, and I just wanted to run back into that hospital and find my baby. But I knew I couldn't. And even if I could, what would I do then? The mommy instinct to protect and hold my baby had been woven into every fiber of my being, but that instinct—that desire—went unfulfilled. What anguish it was to be programmed to do something but not be able to do it. I had no little hands to hold, no cheeks to kiss, no baby to rock. My body physically ached for my baby. The bonding of a momma and baby is incomparable. Even when physically separated, that bond remains intact. What a fierce and powerful love.

The shawl I received in the ER became a constant comfort. I slept with it every night. When the heaviness of my empty arms became too much to endure, I rolled it up and held it. When my body longed for my baby, I wrapped myself in it. The ER bracelets also became something I could touch and look at when I needed to. I wanted anything to keep me close to the memory of that night. Not because I wanted to relive the pain, but because that was the last time that my baby was a part of me. It was the closest I could still be to my baby—both in body and in time. It was all I had left of my baby.

Because we chose to have the hospital take care of final arrangements, we knew it would take a couple months for the funeral home to receive our baby's body. Our hospital partners with a local funeral home that offers their services free of charge to mommies and daddies who have lost babies. What a gloomy service even to think about, until you actually need it. I was so relieved—thankful even—to have that aspect taken care of. My heart couldn't have handled walking through each of those final details.

Finally, the call came. The woman's voice was solemn and reverent. She knew she was talking about sacred life. "We have your sweet baby. We're giving Baby Butler over to the funeral home." That meant our baby's ashes would soon be released at a nearby memorial bench, but to my surprise, I didn't feel an urgency to visit that bench. Initially I felt guilty. But I also realized the timing wasn't right. Knowing that the ashes of my baby would forever be intermingled with the ashes of other precious ones felt like balm to my wounded soul. But I knew their unity didn't end there. These sacred heaven babies were still together, at the feet of my Savior, skipping and playing, dancing and singing with one another.

After we knew our baby's ashes had been spread, I became fearful that others would forget about what had happened, that my baby would become a faded, distant memory to the world. My arm was covered in bruises from blown veins and failed attempts to insert an IV at the ER. They served as a physical reminder of the trauma I had endured. If I could have kept them forever, I would have. I wore the blue and purple marks as a badge, a visual testament. As they began to heal, I felt like I was losing something important. Time was putting more and more distance between me and the last moments I had with my baby. The bruises faded; the memories did not. Even when my arm became less tender, my heart remained sore. Soon the bruises would be gone and I would look "normal" again. But I didn't feel normal. I wasn't ready to feel normal or move on. I wasn't the same person I was before; that little life had branded me forever.

When my body no longer displayed physical testaments

of that night, I began to take solace in my hospital bracelets. I kept them on the kitchen counter so I could look at them whenever I needed. Even if someone came to visit me, I didn't move them. I couldn't bring myself to tuck them away out of sight. I felt as if moving them meant I was ashamed—hiding a piece of my heart, a part of my story. Their function wasn't simply to hold my personal information for medical reasons anymore. They now served as memorial bracelets and remained on my counter for months.

My need to stay connected to my baby was relentless—and the tangible items I did have brought comfort in their own ways. But one evening, as I was standing in my kitchen, something beautiful happened; it was like the fragrance of heaven filled the room. My breath was taken away by the realization that the baby who had been growing on the inside of my body was now on that side of heaven. A life that was inside me, part of my very flesh, was with God! My baby carried a part of my body into the heavenlies straight into the presence of Jesus, and the gap between here and there became less vast. I felt eternity, if only for a moment. Oh, what a beautiful gift—to glimpse into forever and be veiled in heaven's glory. Time was not putting more distance between my baby and me. It was actually bringing us closer together again. There would be a day that I would enter into heaven and see my Lord face to face. There would be a day that I would be reunited with my little one and see his or her face for the first time. I will not be deprived forever of that beautiful sight.

But until then, my baby and my God were together in heaven. And a part of me was there too.

I wrote Scripture on three-by-five-inch cards and taped them all over my home. I used dry-erase markers to write his Word on every mirror and glass surface I could reach. I couldn't get dressed, wash my hands, or even take a shower without seeing Scripture.

One verse that was written in multiple places in my home was Luke 1:45. During the first year I was married, before we had even started trying to have a baby, my heart and mind would struggle with fear and what-ifs. "What if I can't get pregnant? What if I never have children?" I would claim God's promises and combat the fear with verses about God's peace. But one afternoon, I began praying for God to show me a promise in Scripture that was spoken directly to a woman. I yearned for a special Scripture that would speak directly to my feminine soul. I sat on my bed, looking through God's Word, and he graciously gave me the very words my heart so desperately longed to hear.

Blessed is she who has believed that
the Lord would fulfill his promises to her!
Luke 1:45 (NIV)

As I sat on my bed thanking him for that verse, I had no idea that those precious words would become my battle cry a couple years later.

Along with God's Word, the air in my home was constantly swirling with worship music. Every minute of my day was filled with melodious lyrics declaring God's faithfulness and truth. There were moments I would just sit on the sofa and allow my mind to absorb each word, hoping they would trickle down to the depths of my soul. There were times I wanted to pray—that I desperately *needed* to pray to my God—but I lacked any ability to express what I was feeling. I honestly didn't know how I was feeling most of the time. I was sad. So very sad. But I was also angry. Not at God, but just . . . angry. I was confused. I was anxious and broken, yet hopeful. It was everything. I felt everything. When I felt empty and there was nothing left inside of me to pour out, music became my mouthpiece. It became the words I couldn't speak, the prayers I didn't know how to pray, the expression of praise I longed to give to God despite how felt.

I began to realize how powerful it was to look up and say, "Lord, I declare you as faithful *despite* my circumstances. I praise you in *this* moment. I praise you in *this* pain. I know you are a good God and remain good in *this* situation." Some days my heart felt it; other days it didn't. But staying consistent in acknowledging his faithfulness, on both the good days and the bad days, gave me strength and deepened my relationship with him. Being able to say "I don't understand the whys, but I know my God is faithful" was freeing to my heart. I didn't know why I had lost my baby. But my desire to trust him slowly grew stronger than my need to know the whys. And that changed everything for me.

Anneke's Story

I think I was a little worried that people would forget about my babies. There are some friends and family who never asked about it or asked how I was doing with it all. I'm sure they were probably just unsure of what to say, so they didn't say anything. I had one other friend who wanted to do a playdate during my first miscarriage, and she couldn't understand why I wasn't emotionally up to it. She said some very hurtful things that ended up dissolving our friendship.

One of the most helpful things for me was talking through everything with people. I knew some ladies who had experienced loss before, and they were able to walk with me and help with all the hard questions I had. Other ladies who had never experienced miscarriages before were also listening ears and shoulders to cry on during the hardest points. I was very honest about it. When people asked how I was doing with it, and it was a really hard day, I would say that. When they asked if I was praying through it, and I was too angry to pray about it, I would say that too. I knew grieving was a process and that it was healthy to try not to bury the emotions and questions. If anyone offered to pray for me, I always said yes.

Another source that helped while I grieved was worship music. There were a couple of songs that spoke loudly to me about the faithfulness of God even in dark situations and I would listen to them all the time. I knew that left to my own misery, I would become depressed, so I purposefully would listen to those songs and let the words sink in. I ultimately wanted complete healing and full trust in God, so I knew I had to head in that direction.

The last thing that really helped me was getting out, helping people, and serving others. The temptation for me to get too inwardly focused was very great, but I could see that it would be a very dark and lonely path. The most refreshing thing was focusing on others. It actually became a source of healing for me. When you are out serving others, you begin to see how everyone is fighting a battle of some kind and that suffering isn't isolated only to you. So in a way there is a sort of comfort and camaraderie in that. There is another sort of comfort when you know you've been able to be a healing balm to others. Somehow it comes back to you.

Megan's Story

Later in the week, we emailed our family and friends again, this time telling them it was all over. I hated writing it. I didn't want to push the send button, but it was necessary. It was one step towards healing. Talking to friends who had gone through losses helped the most with my immediate healing. My husband was strong and always there for me, and we rejoiced that our daughter was in heaven and grieved that she wasn't with us. Our little girl was real. We were fortunate to see her with our own eyes. We gave her the name Eliana. It means "my God has answered." He answers our prayers in many ways—sometimes in ways we don't like or in ways that don't make sense to us, but he remains good and we must have faith in that.

My heart was hurting, my body was aching with the emptiness, and my eyes were blinded by emotions. At first it seemed my husband jumped right back into the daily routine of life, work, and normalcy. He went in to work the day after our baby had been born, and I was a little sad because of it, wishing he would be home with our daughter and me. I wanted to be angry with him for not "taking time" to mourn, as if nothing ever happened. What I didn't realize until later, though, was that it really did affect him. It really impacted him when he got to see and hold tiny Eliana in his hand after I delivered her. I've always heard it said that a woman feels she becomes a mother as soon as she knows she's pregnant, and a man feels he becomes a father when he holds his baby in his arms for the first time. I believe it was true for him that day.

My husband was a rock for me in those hard weeks, but I also know it was God's special care to put certain women in my life during that time—women whom I needed and who needed me. We supported each other in our losses in ways that our husbands couldn't. I know that's exactly what God intended for each of us in those moments. The Scripture verse that helped me the most was Hebrews 11:1–3: "Now faith is the substance of things hoped for, the evidence of things not seen. For by it the elders obtained a good testimony. By faith we understand that the worlds were framed by the word of God, so that the things which are seen were not made of things which are visible" (NKJV).

I had a few ultrasound pictures of Eliana, from our first ultrasound, that comforted me. I kept them by my bed for a while. I felt a little worried that people would forget about Eliana. And I suppose I still feel somewhat at odds with my thoughts when I do bring her up. I always wonder if people think it's strange that I call her by name, or that I even named her. However, I always talk about her anyway, even if I get surprised looks from others when I mention her by name. I just don't want to forget her, or those close to me to forget her.

Years later I feel I am still healing from losing a child. Being able to talk about Eliana is healing. And being a listening ear to those who are going through a miscarriage is also healing.

God's Promise

For you formed my inward parts;
you knitted me together in my mother's womb.
I praise you, for I am fearfully and wonderfully made.
Wonderful are your works;
my soul knows it very well.
My frame was not hidden from you,
when I was being made in secret,
intricately woven in the depths of the earth.
Your eyes saw my unformed substance;
in your book were written, every one of them,
the days that were formed for me,
when as yet there was none of them.
Psalm 139:13–16 (ESV)

Prayer

My faithful God,

My heart aches so deeply. My body yearns for my baby. My mind battles fear and anxiety. There are some moments I feel as if I will succumb to the brokenness. Your truth is the only thing that transcends the depth of my fragility. Help me to trust you, moment by moment. Show me how to praise you continually despite how my emotions waver. Thank you for my baby's life and for the beautiful mark that is forever branded on my soul. In Jesus's name, amen.

Journal

Before even you knew you were pregnant, God knew you had life inside of you, and he holds great value in that precious life. Matthew 10:29–31 says, "Are not two sparrows sold for a penny? And not one of them will fall to the ground apart from your Father. But even the hairs of your head are all numbered. Fear not, therefore; you are of more value than many sparrows" (ESV). Although the time was far too short by human standards, God was intricately creating your child within you. He knew whether your child would be a girl or boy, have your eyes, your husband's hair color. Your baby branded you. And you will forever bear the mark that testifies to your baby's life. You are the mother to that child, and your heart will always remember and treasure your baby's life.

How has your baby's life transformed your life? Has this changed the way you view God, yourself, others, and the world in general? In what ways are your mind, body, and heart branded by your baby's life?

CHAPTER THREE

exposed

There is no foot too small that it cannot leave an imprint on this world.
—Unknown

Over the next few weeks, I stayed home. Jarred ran all the errands. He picked up the groceries. He talked to people so I didn't have to. He did everything. I went out only once with him to get some dinner. And even then, I just wanted to go through a drive-through somewhere so I didn't have to interact in any capacity with another human. It was strange to me that everyone was acting so normal. I almost found insult with the fact that the world was going about its business when my entire world had been violently shaken and knocked off its axis. Surely, they had felt the earthquake from my heart breaking that night. How could the entire world look so different without them noticing as well? But as we drove around and I saw people shopping, driving, talking, and living as usual, I realized they didn't know. How could they have, really? I suppose the destruction from the shock waves went inward. Still, it was odd that I felt so different when the outward world hadn't changed. They didn't know. They didn't know how broken I was or how strange the air now tasted to me. And it was lonely.

My heart encapsulated a sacred secret: one worth telling, but one worth guarding as well. It was too precious to share with just anyone. I think that's why I stayed home for weeks, not setting foot anywhere I could be seen or, worse yet, talked to. If someone asked me how my baby was doing, I would have to tell them. And then I would have to endure the looks of sympathy and words that didn't fix anything and responses that I didn't have control over. If they asked, I'd have to say . . . something. But I wasn't ready for many others to hold that tender secret along with me. We had told our friends and family, but it was easy not to answer phone calls or respond to text messages. Seeing someone face-to-face left me completely exposed. No ignoring. No wall. No hiding. No buffer. Absolutely no control.

The idea of having to say, "we lost the baby," over and over filled my grieving heart with anxiety. My stomach knotted up, and my heart felt like it was being choked. I could physically feel the discomfort, fear, and dread of being around other people grip me. I had made it to the "safe" part of my pregnancy, so we had shared our news with *everyone*. People at church. People at

Jarred's work. Our neighbors. Heck, even our regular cashiers at the grocery store knew. So many people knew. Including Vicki.

Vicki lived in the same apartment complex as we did. Up until I lost the baby, Jarred and I would take our dog for a walk at the same time every day. As we turned the corner on our street, I knew Vicki would most likely be sitting on her porch, smoking a cigarette. Even in the middle of summer she wore a black winter coat while she sat outside so the smoke wouldn't permeate her clothes. The first time we met Vicki we talked to her for what felt like forever. She was the kind of person who instantly made you feel like you had been her friend for years, even though you had just learned each other's names minutes earlier. She told us that she had three kids, one of them a newborn. She laid out the long and detailed history of how she ended up living in that apartment, and then gave us the rundown of neighborhood happenings. She even ran inside to grab ultrasound pictures of her baby boy whom she had just given birth to. She was genuinely happy for us when we told her we were pregnant and even offered baby clothes to us if our little one was a boy.

After voluntarily confining myself to our apartment for a few weeks, I began missing our daily walks together. It had always been a time for my husband and me to talk, reconnect, and just breathe fresh air. I especially enjoyed walking past the patios that displayed large ceramic planters spilling over with brightly colored blossoms and thriving foliage. Each time we walked by, the fragrances easily coaxed my feet to slow their pace just so I could linger in the sweet air. I missed that. So when my body felt physically better, we started walking the dog together again. Only now we would skip over Vicki's street because I knew she would ask me how I was feeling and how the baby was doing, just like she had done every time before. And I just didn't have it in me to see her. I felt like after I told Vicki we had lost our baby, everything would be set into motion and I would have to tell the rest of the world. She represented a doorway that led to the outside world. If I didn't tell her—if I kept that door shut—my heart wouldn't be exposed and I wouldn't have to face the harsh climate on the other side. As long as I could delay that step, my lips wouldn't repeatedly have to form those four painful words, "We lost the baby." I don't know which I dreaded more, telling people or anticipating their responses. I didn't know how people would react or what they would say. But to be honest, I didn't know how *I* would react or what *I* would say. Maybe that's what I was scared of. There were moments I wished I could have stayed tucked away forever like some fragile, pain-filled princess in a tall, dark tower.

But no matter where I tried to hide, Jesus always met me there. The sweetness of his presence offered solace when feelings of isolation threatened to ensnare me. Jesus brought my despondent heart a little more life each day. And every morning, my weary soul woke up with a little more strength. One afternoon as my husband was getting the dog leashed and ready for our walk, I thought about which route we would take. I hadn't even considered going down Vicki's street the previous weeks, so my hesitation caught me off guard. Was I ready to see her . . . and *talk* to her? I didn't feel ready per se, but I knew eventually I would have to talk to her. I would have to reenter into the world, no matter how exposed I felt. And for some reason, in that moment, my courage pressed me on.

"Let's go down Vicki's street today."

The moment those words came out of my mouth, my heart began pounding. I told my husband that I felt panicky—intimidated in a way—to talk to her. He reassured me that I was not alone and that we would make it a quick chat. We headed downstairs from our second-story apartment and began our family stroll down our street. Only this time when we got to the end of the sidewalk, we turned right—down Vicki's street. *Maybe she isn't outside and I won't have to talk to her. Or maybe we should just turn around. It's not too late to go back.* I stopped for a moment to take a few deep breaths to see if that little piece of bravery I felt inside our apartment was also here outside with me. And sure enough, within the trembling hands and shaky voice, it was still pressing through. As we rounded the street corner, there she was. Vicki was sitting on her porch, cigarette in hand. As soon as she saw us down at the other end of the street, she stood up and began waving her arms. The walk down that long sidewalk was so awkward. After we got close enough to talk to, she said with excitement, "I haven't seen you guys in weeks! Have you been out of town?" And then without taking a breath or giving us time to answer her first questions, she asked, "How are you? How's the baby doing?"

"We lost the baby."

The smile that had covered her entire face immediately melted away. I'll never forget her response. "Oh, sh*t. I am so . . . so sorry." Maybe it was because her words were so unfiltered and genuine; maybe it was because her raw word choice was exactly how I felt about it all; I couldn't help but grin. "Vicki, your response is probably the most accurate to how I've felt. Thank you."

And sweet, talkative Vicki didn't miss a beat and began sharing some stories of women in her life who had also lost babies. It was comforting to hear about some of the details of other women's losses. I knew I hurt, I knew I felt broken, I knew I ached for my baby—but I was not alone. An entire sisterhood was out there of women I had never even met. Vicki's stories came to a close. I thanked her for her kindness and assured her that she'd be seeing a lot of us again. We started to make our way back to our apartment. When we were almost to the end of the sidewalk, I heard Vicki yell, "And remember, you're really fertile next month!"

Oh, Vicki. You were exactly what I needed.

The knocking down of the dominoes line was set into motion, and I felt like life after loss had begun. Living my new normal had begun. I was back in the world.

The following week I went to visit Jarred at the ministry organization he worked for. I was so delighted to see him in his element, getting a glimpse of that part of his daily life. I was thankful Jarred had sent out an organization-wide email the day after we lost the baby so that I didn't have to be the news giver. As I began walking around and saying hello to familiar faces, I watched as their expressions turned from a normal smile to sympathy. It was wonderful and uncomfortable at the same time. I appreciated their tenderness. I appreciated their concern. Some of the women hugged me, asking how I was doing and feeling. Some shared about the losses that their daughters had experienced. Others cried with me and told me about their own losses—one that happened eighteen years before. Their stories served as proof that time did not heal all wounds—not completely. The tears still flowed freely and unaltered despite the years gone by. My husband and I were not the only inhabitants in the desolate land of baby loss. The more we shared our story, the more it was affirmed over and over. Stories of losses that were tucked away deep inside of the women and men I talked to were brought to the surface that day—and the healing power of camaraderie gained more ground inside of us. Loss bound us, empathy bonded us, and our unspoken sisterhood united us.

Visiting a group setting at Jarred's office had been a big step for me. But it was just that, a step. There were many more to go—one of them being a social function where friends and acquaintances would attend. As someone who prefers a quiet evening at home over spending any extended amount of time in large crowds, my stomach always flips as I walk into parties or large gatherings. But this stomach flop was extra floppy. I would have to be social *and* talk about my loss. Up until the moment I touched the doorknob, I second-guessed my ability to endure such a vulnerable situation. And to my dismay, no sudden burst of confidence or flood of bravery filled my fluttery heart after I turned the knob and opened the door. I was relieved when my initial entrance didn't feel as cumbersome as I had anticipated. We were among the first to arrive. *Maybe I can do this. Maybe it won't be as weird as I thought.* Then more people began trickling in, and I quickly began feeling like a wounded animal roaming around the room. The sympathetic "Aww, poor girl" looks killed me. I felt as exposed as the classic standing-in-the-middle-of-a-crowded-room-completely-naked dream, except a hundred times worse. It wasn't embarrassing; it was just painful. The only thing that made it worse was when the glances came from pregnant women. They felt awkward because they had life growing inside of them. I felt awkward because I didn't. They didn't know what to say. I didn't know what to say. So we didn't say anything at all.

The evening finally ended, and I had survived. I saw people and I even talked to them. My flat tummy shared a room with round tummies. And I survived.

Each person, each story, each outing brought me a little more confidence to take another step further into the world. Each time, my new normal became more normal. I hadn't thought it was possible, but the paralyzing fear of my grieving heart being completely exposed to others started to lessen. The movement was slow, but it was still movement.

Amy's Story

At first, it was very lonely. Even my sweet man, who was so comforting, could not fully understand what I was experiencing. I think for men, a lot of the time, pregnancy is fairly intangible because their body is not connected to the baby from the beginning. But I was shocked at how many women I knew, and considered dear, who had been through the same thing. And that I didn't know. It can be such a silent grief. It was so comforting to me to know they knew. They brought meals. They sat with me. They cried with me. They didn't really have to say much. I felt so cared for by God through his daughters.

We were a part of a small group at the time who had been praying with us. The night we joined the group, we had just found out that things weren't normal with our baby. I hesitated to share when it came time to pray, but I sensed God's spirit nudging me to share. This is how community is built, after all. The group leader very tenderly let me know that I was in good company and that they would pray. These couples had more babies with Jesus than alive on earth. I was overwhelmed.

Keri's Story

I didn't feel isolated in my loss and grief, mainly because all of my sisters lost babies around the same time. However, I did feel a little alone on Mother's Day because it was just a few weeks after my first loss. But even on Mother's Day I sat next to one of my best friends who had had a miscarriage before having their little son. This was supposed to be her "victory!" Mother's Day, but instead she held her son and cried with me.

Talking to other women helped a lot. I am a total extrovert, and I immediately told our life group and some of our church leaders that we were pregnant so that they could pray for us. I was so glad that I had told them, because when we lost our baby they came alongside of us in our pain and supported us in many ways. They knew how to love us because they knew what we were going through. I know people are different in this way and there is not one way to go about it. But I was thankful that we told them.

God's Promise

Be strong and courageous. Do not be afraid; do not be discouraged, for the LORD your God will be with you wherever you go.
Joshua 1:9 (NIV)

A Prayer

My God,

The world is an intimidating place to me right now. Some of the people I will see and the conversations I will have feel too painful and too intimate to face. There are days I just want to stay in bed and hide away forever. Nothing feels the same or looks like it did before I lost my baby. And more than anything, I am not the same. My baby will always be a part of my life, my story, and my heart—but reentering the world with that beautiful tenderness scares me right now. Please remind me of truth when the world discourages me. Thank you, Jesus. In your name, amen.

Journal

Wondering how the world will react to your loss can be overwhelming when your grief is still raw and emotions sometimes feel unpredictable. Anticipating people's reactions can be emotionally draining on its own, and enduring the comments and situations you dread can leave you feeling exposed and fragile. You can have confidence knowing that God is with you wherever you go and he will always be the shelter you can take refuge in. God's word says, "Be merciful to me, O God, be merciful to me, for in you my soul takes refuge; in the shadow of your wings I will take refuge, till the storms of destruction pass by" (Ps. 57:1 ESV).

What is your biggest concern as you talk to people, go back to work, let others hear about your loss, etc.? As you begin to enter back into your "normal" life routine, what are some boundaries you can put in place to protect your heart and emotions?

CHAPTER FOUR

words

A wife who loses a husband is called a widow. A husband who loses a wife is called a widower. A child who loses his parents is called an orphan. There is no word for a parent who loses a child. That's how awful the loss is.
—Ronald Reagan

Even after I began to feel physically stronger, I think the main reason I wanted to stay locked in my house was because I remained emotionally frail. I dreaded the responses of others towards my loss because I knew their words, whether healing or hurtful, would pierce my heart. Would their piercing words infuse my heart with life and healing, or would they leave me feeling more broken and sorrowful than before? The only way to find out was to hear them. And that notion was almost too much to anticipate. So I limited my interaction with the outside world.

I was very fortunate to be surrounded by tender, sensitive people who were careful with their words. They guarded my heart and protected my process of grieving. However, grief is an unpredictable thing, and it left me feeling unpredictable at times too. Careless words were potential arrows, and my heart was this huge, unmissable target that would surely be struck over and over. Even well-intentioned or innocently given statements had the ability to sting. In the moments where I felt especially vulnerable, simple comments such as "it will get better" or "one day it won't hurt as bad" left me hurt—angry even. Some days I didn't want to feel better. Some days I didn't want the pain to lessen because that pain was the most tangible thing I had left. Allowing the grief to wrap around me and squeeze me tightly was almost comforting.

Being around people who knew about my loss made my heart feel unprotected, like my grief was on display. I repeatedly climbed to extreme highs and tumbled to severe lows. And there were moments when my emotions experienced something similar to that of being thrown inside a washing machine turned to a tsunami setting—a violent swishing and swashing with no way to know which way was up and which way was down. All I could do was try to keep my head above the agitating water, try to take my next breath, and then prepare myself as I inevitably got pulled back under. I was frustrated that outside words dictated my emotions so easily. I could make an intentional effort to prepare myself for what could possibly be said, but the moment I heard a hurtful comment spoken aloud, I crumbled like a frail graham cracker in the hands of an unwieldy toddler.

Some words were triggering. Some words were hurtful. Some words were wonderful. But no matter which way I cut it, every word impacted me to some degree.

There are so many different scenarios or comments that you may experience after a loss. A few common ones can be particularly prickly . . .

"I'm pregnant!"

One punch that knocked the air out of me came from others' pregnancy announcements. Whether it was a direct text from a friend or a general post of an ultrasound picture on social media, it devastated me. Hearing someone else's joyful news would bring me to my knees. But not for the reason that most would think. Reading happy statuses of pregnancy proclamations reminded me of what I had just lost. Hearing excited voices eagerly shout out their news to the world reminded me of the mournful shouts I released into those dark nights. It felt impossible that my heart should be able to split right down the middle, but split it did: one side of my heart empty, barely beating with grief and loss, and the other side full of life and pumping with happiness for expectant family and friends. What a conflicted state to dwell in. My pain wasn't directly correlated to their happy news; the timing was just hard. Who are we kidding, the whole situation was hard. But as difficult as it was to separate my own sadness from the happiness I felt for the pregnant ones I loved, it was exponentially difficult to congratulate others who seemed indifferent—unhappy even—about their pregnancies. I begrudgingly endured the ones who were filled with annoyance or disappointment of "having to be pregnant again." Between the two of us, how was I the one who *wanted* to be pregnant but wasn't? My mind couldn't wrap itself around that unfair fact. Such a cruel truth.

Distancing yourself from certain people or disconnecting from social media altogether—even if for a short period—can be helpful in creating an emotional safe haven for yourself. If you need to step away from a commitment that would be too hard to endure, do it. If you need to kindly decline invitations to baby showers, birthday parties, or other triggering gatherings, do it. Allow yourself time and space to breathe and grieve. People will usually understand if you're not ready to attend parties or get-togethers, especially events where there will be pregnant women, babies, or people whom you just aren't ready to see. Of course, there will be *that* person who just can't understand why you're unable to jump right back into life as before. And although you won't be able to avoid every difficult person or painful pregnancy announcement, you can establish boundaries that create a safe space where you are allowed to feel whatever you need to feel. Surround yourself with supportive friends, decline invitations as needed, unfollow people on social media or take a break from it altogether. Your heart and healing are what matter, and the path to getting there looks different for each of us.

"God has better plans."

It's seems to be easy for others to tell you that God is in control or that he has better plans when they aren't the ones whose baby died. They usually mean it to be comforting. When someone told me, after I shared my loss story with this person, that "God has better plans," I felt my face become flush with frustration and hurt. How dare they tell me God has better plans for me than for my baby to live. Did my baby's life not make the cut? Did God make a mistake? I wholeheartedly believe that God is sovereign. I believe he is in control. I believe he sees every baby being woven together in his or her mother's womb. I believe he forms each of their little bodies and knows and loves each one of them fiercely (Ps. 139:13). I believe his ways and thoughts are higher than mine (Isa. 55:9). But telling me that God has better plans in response to a loss sounds like my baby's life was taken away in order for "better" plans to be carried out. Not only is that absurd, it's untrue and hurtful.

I believe God is Almighty and that he has complete power over all things. But I don't believe God caused my miscarriages. As much as I wish I did understand, I don't. I don't know why babies die or are allowed to die. I just don't. But what I do know is this: I have lost two babies, and both times, the Lord did not leave me. There were moments when his presence felt faint. There were moments I felt confused and angry. But at the core of all that, he was there. He was there grieving alongside me. He walked alongside me. He carried me when I could barely lift my head or say a prayer. His Word, his presence was and is water to my dry soul. And that is how I know he is still good and that his plans for me are good.

"Are you going to try again?"

"I'm sorry for your loss. Are you going to try again?" I was faced with that question repeatedly as I told people we had lost our baby. Many times I thought, *Gee, thanks. Do you at least want to take a breath in between those two sentences?* When a person's response to my loss came in the form of the question "Are you going to try again?" it made me feel like my baby's life was being dismissed or could easily be replaced. I didn't feel like it was others' business to ask that question—especially not people who didn't know us well.

"Trying again" is not about replacing your baby, and it doesn't mean you have forgotten your baby. That desire—that deep ache and longing to have a baby—doesn't minimize your loss or your pain, and it definitely doesn't minimize your baby's life. Your heaven baby will always be your baby.

Are you going to try again? Maybe your answer is *yes*, maybe your answer is *no*, maybe your answer is *not right now*, maybe your answer is *I can't.* Whatever your answer is, it's yours, not the world's. Grief does not fit a cookie-cutter shape, so walk in the direction your body and heart are calling you towards. It can be overwhelming even to think past today. Whether you feel like you have a clear plan to the future, or you feel like your whole world is spinning out of control, the Lord knows what tomorrow looks like. Proverbs 16:9 says, "We can make our plans, but the LORD determines our steps" (NLT). Take heart, you are being cared for.

"My friend had a miscarriage; I know how you feel."

No, no you don't. You've had an up close view, but it was still from the outside looking in. Unless you've experienced loss yourself, you don't know how I feel. You don't understand what it feels like to have empty arms that are so heavy it feels impossible to hold them up. Arms that long to hold your baby but are unable to. You don't understand what it's like to break down in the middle of the day without any warning—mourning and crying so hard and heavy that you feel like you will pass out or throw up.

No matter how hard a person tries to understand what we're going through, if they have never lost a baby, they can't understand. Not fully. And even though I have lost babies myself, I don't know *exactly* how another momma is feeling. Each of us is so different. We all grieve differently, in our own time, in our own ways. Our situations are different. The details of our losses are all different. So, while I lovingly support you, momma, and stand with you in unity in our sisterhood of loss, I acknowledge that our journeys are different and that I don't know exactly how you feel.

"Thank goodness you weren't further along."

This one is a stinger. Like the level of grief you're allowed to experience is dependent on how far along you were. Nonsense. Whether you lost your baby as soon as you found out you were pregnant or you were months along, you still lost your baby. The details of each story are different, but each story shares a common core—loss.

From the moment we see those two pink lines on a pregnancy test, the planning begins—the hopes and dreams we have for the child are in full swing. So it doesn't matter how far along you were in your pregnancy when you lost a baby—you lost a baby. The physical pain, the procedures, the process may vary. But your baby is real. The loss is real. The grief is real. There is no "thank goodness."

When nothing is said.

I quickly realized that the most hurtful responses I received were silent ones. At first, the emails and calls and messages poured in. My heart and inbox overflowed with comforting and kind words. But slowly, like a faucet being turned off, the concerns and messages and texts lessened . . . until they became a trickle. And sometimes, it felt like there was nothing at all. Months after my loss, I wished that people would ask me how I was doing. There were those few friends who weren't afraid to bring up my loss and would ask me how I was doing. But they were few. There were many times I would see a friend for the first time after my loss and nothing would be said. The silence smothered me. I knew they were aware that I had lost a baby. But still, there was silence. Why? Why was nothing said?

Before I had experienced loss myself, when I heard that a friend lost a baby, it was easy to make that initial call or send that initial message and express how sorry I was. However, after a little time passed, I realized how uncomfortable and unsure I felt asking her about how she was doing. What if she was having a good day and I brought up her loss? I didn't want to make her sad or cause her to relive her loss. I didn't want to burden her with that heaviness. So I wouldn't say anything else. I regret those times because I now know how agonizing and isolating the silence is.

As mommas who have lost babies, we are painfully aware of our losses every single moment of every single day. We don't get the option of moving forward in life unaffected. We don't get the option of being distracted or forgetting. Not that we would even want to. None of us can forget our babies or remain unchanged. Whether or not someone mentions our losses or asks how we are doing, we are aware of what happened. Sometimes it is so very lonely when others hesitate to enter into that place with us. Even the simplest of acknowledgments can be healing for our hearts. A simple

"I'm so sorry" has the ability to soothe a wounded heart. Mentioning our babies' lives or names is powerful—to know that the world has not forgotten about them, or us. It reminds us that our losses are real. Real children. Real grief. Real pain.

I'm sure you've heard the old adage "Sticks and stones may break my bones, but words can never hurt me." Really? Can I please talk to whoever came up with that adorable, catchy little lie? Don't get me wrong, it's a nice idea—this concept of not being affected by what others say to us. But it's just not possible. Not entirely anyway. And I don't think that's a negative thing. Words are meant to hold power. They are meant to be given graciously and to bring healing to hurting hearts and fresh air to weary lungs. But not every speaker is filled with grace or wisdom or even love. God's Word repeatedly tells us, and even warns us, about the power that words can have. But words don't have to be true in order to impact or hurt the recipient. You and I know that, don't we? Okay, so now what? We know words hold power, but we can't stop others from speaking. So how do we guard our hearts from words without becoming a hermit and living under a rock in the middle of the woods? I believe the answer to that question lies in this statement: *God's Word is the final word in my life.*

We do not have to allow our hearts and minds to absorb, passively and willingly, everything that is spoken to us.

The negative or hurtful words that our hearts hear louder than our ears should not go unchallenged! Meaning, challenge those lies. Challenge the deceit that the enemy is spewing. Speak the truth aloud against them. While others' words have the *potential* to affect us negatively, God's Word holds *exponential* power for our lives.

You hold a fierceness inside of you, dear momma. You are a warrior, even when you feel broken. I would even say, you are a warrior *because* you feel broken—because you carry your brokenness while still placing one foot in front of the other each day. Is a warrior's armor perfectly polished and untouched? No. A warrior's armor is beat up. It is dented and marked and testifies to the blows and attacks it has endured. The warrior's body itself bears the marks and scars of the battles that have been fought. Yes, you are a warrior of the heart, dear one. And the victory is yours. Do not let the enemy tell you otherwise.

The truth that God speaks about us is *the* ultimate truth in its fullest measure and deepest degree. His words are insurmountably more powerful and life-giving than any word that passes over human lips. That is why it is vital to take hold of the truth and repeat it *aloud* whenever negative, hurtful, or careless words attempt to penetrate our minds and hearts. When lies from the enemy start to swirl in your thoughts, rebuke them *aloud* and speak truth *aloud*. When the seemingly harmless residual effect of a hurtful comment starts to take root in your heart, uproot it *aloud* with God's truth! When verbal swords threaten your sense of peace, hope, or healing, combat them *aloud* with your own Scripture-filled sword.

> *For the word of God is living and active, sharper than any two-edged sword, piercing to the division of soul and of spirit, of joints and of marrow, and discerning the thoughts and intentions of the heart.*
> Hebrews 4:12 (ESV)

The God of the universe created you. The God of the universe loves you with an everlasting love. The God of the universe sent his only Son to die on a cross for *you*! That's how treasured and loved and precious you are to him! Zephaniah 3:17 says that "the LORD your God is in your midst, a mighty one who will save; he will rejoice over you with gladness; he will quiet you by his love; he will exult over you with loud singing" (ESV). Those are words of truth to claim and speak and declare aloud. They are for you. *He* is for you.

Matthew 12:36 says, "I tell you, on the day of judgment people will give account for every careless word they speak" (ESV).

Proverbs 16:24 says, "Gracious words are like a honeycomb, sweetness to the soul and health to the body" (ESV).

Proverbs 18:21 says, "Death and life are in the power of the tongue, and those who love it will eat its fruits" (ESV).

Anneke's Story

After one of my losses, a person said they wondered what God was trying to teach me through my losses. I was taken aback at first because I didn't view God like that. I couldn't bring myself to believe that he was the sort who would smite me with that kind of pain just to teach me a lesson. I fully believed that he would use it for some kind of good and that good would ultimately come out of it, but not that he was the source of pain and death. However, I knew that this person meant it as a comfort and not as an insult. I would much rather that they talked with me about it instead of avoiding conversation about it altogether. I would have found that more hurtful. Also, years later, I have to say my theology on the topic is not hard-set. During all the times of asking God the painful whys, he always very clearly and gently answered, "Anneke, trust me." The thought at one time that he would make me go down that path on purpose was a very bitter thought. I think now if I found out that was the case (as in the book of Job), I could handle it, because I have tasted of him and found that he is good and faithful and perfect in his love.

Erin's Story

I experienced insensitive comments after my loss. I still do. People generally like to compare painful incidents, like "mine is worse" or "it has to be worse giving birth and losing your baby versus losing your baby just during pregnancy." But that discounts my experience as insignificant or less painful. This happens a lot, even to this day, a handful of years later. I cannot say whether or not one experience is better or worse than the other as far as painfulness is concerned, but I can say that people tend to compare instead of just listen. If I feel compelled to share my story, I'm often interrupted in the middle of sharing with "Oh yes, I totally understand. I had a miscarriage too." But no, you don't understand. Because what I went through and a miscarriage are two very different things. When people compare painful stories, it's hurtful and insensitive.

The first couple of years after my loss were really difficult. I would get angry when I would see pregnant teenage girls or hear people complain about their pregnancies. I wanted what they had so bad. With friends, it was easier to be happy for them, but it was still difficult. I would cry and cry seeing their expanding bellies, being so envious, bitter, and angry that I couldn't get pregnant. It was very hard and took a toll on me, my marriage, and my friendships. Thankfully God restores and over time those feeling got better. Now, a handful of years later, I can genuinely be happy for a friend or family member who is pregnant, but if I'm honest, even now when I hear them complain about their pregnancies, I feel that deep burning feeling of hurt seeping up, and I whisper in my head, *Just be happy you're able to get pregnant!* It's a struggle and one that changes over time. It can be a roller coaster of emotion in that regard. Some years it's better, some years it's not as good, but God's hand is always there to hold mine through the valleys.

God's Promise

And the peace of God, which transcends all understanding, will guard your hearts and your minds in Christ Jesus.

Finally, brothers and sisters, whatever is true, whatever is noble, whatever is right, whatever is pure, whatever is lovely, whatever is admirable—if anything is excellent or praiseworthy—think about such things. Whatever you have learned or received or heard from me, or seen in me—put it into practice. And the God of peace will be with you.
Philippians 4:7–9 (NIV)

A Prayer

Lord Jesus,

Please guard my heart and mind from hurtful words and actions of others. Whether others' words are intentionally hurtful or simply carelessly spoken, both can inflict such pain on my already vulnerable heart. Help me to absorb only what is beautiful and truth-filled. Remind me that I do not have to claim or accept any negative, hurtful, or untrue words. Above anyone's words, your words hold the truth that defines me and reveals whom you have created me to be. Thank you for the promises you have given to me. Thank you for the healing you speak into my brokenness. I claim this in Jesus's name, amen.

Journal

Whether the words you hear come from an outward source, your own mouth, or internal self-talk, you can choose which words to hold onto.

Singing worship music to God, speaking Scripture, praying, and claiming truth aloud strengthens and empowers your spirit and can cultivate a new boldness and confidence inside of you! This is vital when rejecting lies from the enemy and replacing them with the truth from your God. Not one word of truth we speak is hollow. Each one of them holds power and life.

> *For as the rain and the snow come down from heaven*
> *and do not return there but water the earth,*
> *making it bring forth and sprout,*
> *giving seed to the sower and bread to the eater,*
> *so shall my word be that goes out from my mouth;*
> *it shall not return to me empty,*
> *but it shall accomplish that which I purpose,*
> *and shall succeed in the thing for which I sent it.*
> Isaiah 55:10–11 (ESV)

What Scripture verse can you speak aloud and hold onto when others' words or actions shake you? Write that verse in multiple places of your house, workplace, or even car. When fear or anger or confusion begin to grip your heart, declare the truth of that verse for yourself. Sometimes your emotions have to catch up to the truth-filled words you speak, so even when you do not *feel* it, still *speak* it.

CHAPTER FIVE

longing

Mother is a verb. It's something you do. Not just who you are.
—Cheryl Lacey Donovan

Trying again. I wasn't sure why that term was unsettling to me, but it was. I deeply longed to grow our family, and I did want to have a healthy baby but "trying again" sounded inaccurate. It was void of emotion or pain or history. Like I had failed at something and just needed a redo. It felt like my loss was something I could clear off the board and try for something successful this time around. *Oh, that pregnancy didn't work out, so I'll just try again.*

At first, everyday actions felt forced and disjointed. But each new day brought along with it more clarity about what my new normal looked like. Getting into a new routine after my loss was a process, but eventually the motions felt more fluid. My heart began to settle into a place of peace, and I realized that moving forward with my life didn't mean I was leaving my heaven baby behind. It meant I would stand up from the tear-soaked ground that I had been lying on and I would walk. And as I walked, I would carry my baby's life with me. My baby would be in every beat of my heart, every breath passing through my lungs. Each step I took forward left a footprint that bore witness to where I had been—and gave evidence to the journey I was traveling. As I began to live life intentionally again, I found myself forging a path through unknown terrain.

As I talked to my midwife about physical recovery and emotional healing, she suggested that I wait at least a year to get pregnant again. Her words were like iron weights wrapped around my already heavy heart, as if it could sink any lower. I valued her concern and professional opinion, but her very specific time line didn't feel right for me. I had a follow-up appointment with an obstetrician scheduled for the following week, and I decided I wanted a second opinion. I spent the days leading up to my appointment thinking about how it would play out. I longed for words of comfort. I just wanted to be told that everything was going to be okay. I longed for encouragement from a medical standpoint. But what if I was told the same thing that my midwife expressed—that I did need to wait a year to get pregnant? I thoroughly considered each of the emotions that that answer would bring: fear, anxiety, anger, devastation. I envisioned myself sitting in the patient room, talking with the doctor. I wondered which of the hypothetical movies playing in my head would be accurate to the actual appointment.

Finally, the day of the appointment arrived. As I walked into the office, my stomach was fluttering with butterflies. I had anticipated this appointment for a week, which doesn't sound like a long time—unless you can understand how every hour of every day was a constant replaying of scenarios in my head and nonstop considerations about how the dialogue would affect my mind and heart and life. Waiting a week was a long, long time. The waiting area itself was beautiful, peaceful. I was called back to a room where my husband and I waited some more. My nurse, Julie, came in, and I immediately knew that she was one of the kindest people I had ever met. Her long blonde hair framed her constantly smiling face. As captivated as I was with her entire demeanor, I was drawn to her heart from the moment she walked into the room.

I'd be perfectly content saying that I randomly scheduled an appointment with Julie. But if I'm going to be completely honest with how I discovered her, it's a little unconventional. And embarrassing. And maybe a little weird. Since I had been seeing a midwife prior, the task of finding a new ob-gyn was overwhelming. I really didn't even know where to begin. I read through reviews online about different doctors' offices. I asked friends for suggestions. I tried to research as much as I could.

But it was exhausting, and there didn't seem to be an explicit answer. So, I went with the method I use for choosing a new hairstylist when moving to a new town. I went online, found the website for each office, and then the staff page. I then proceeded to scroll down pictures of the doctors and nurses. When I got to Julie's picture, I decided she looked like someone I would want to be friends with. She was lovely and had kind eyes, and I could envision us having coffee together. I knew we wouldn't *actually* ever have coffee together, but I could still envision it.

She was a perfect fit to my very scientific, methodical criteria, so I made an appointment with her. She sat and talked with me and my husband. She was detailed, unrushed, and tender. So tender. She answered our questions, and even though I knew she had talked to many women before me who had also lost babies, I didn't feel like a statistic. I wasn't "just another one." She was genuinely sympathetic and addressed each of our concerns. Our conversation was open and real and raw. It was so nice to talk about everything with no filter. There was no awkwardness, no embarrassment, no discomfort. What a gift that conversation was. I told her that my midwife suggested we wait a year to get pregnant again and that we wanted to start trying to get pregnant again as soon as I was physically healed enough to do so. She told me as long as I was physically healed and felt ready emotionally, there was no medical reason to wait a full year. The moment her lips released those words, my entire body took a deep breath of relief and hope. I began to feel even more confident in our desire to get pregnant again.

There was a longing in the deepest realms of my soul. It fueled my intense desire to be called Momma. Motherhood invited me to keep living, keep moving. In the still moments, the enemy immediately tried to ensnare my mind with thoughts of "this could happen again" and "you won't be able to get pregnant." The fact was, no matter what my own desires were, I knew that the opposite could happen. I had just experienced that. But through my own shattered plan, I witnessed the unwavering, unchanging, unfaltering steadfastness of my God. His faithfulness flowed deeper than the raging waters of brokenness. His presence outreached fear. His peace covered wounds and healed.

Once again, just as I had done during the early years of our marriage, our entire apartment became a canvas on which I wrote Luke 1:45: "Blessed is she who has believed that the Lord would fulfill his promises to her!" (NIV). I used dry-erase markers to write that verse on every mirror. I wrote it backwards on the glass door of my shower so I could see it when I bathed. I wrote it on index cards and pinned them on walls, laid them next to my bed, and taped them on cabinet doors in my kitchen. I knew whatever happened, the Lord would remain with me. And no matter where I was in my home, those words were there reminding and ensuring me of

God's promises and faithfulness.

My body felt healed. I was thankful for some degree of physical normalcy again. About six weeks after I lost my baby, I had a normal period. I have never been so elated to go buy tampons and a bottle of ibuprofen! I swore from that time on I would never speak negatively about my period. It was no longer just an annoying week to get through; it now symbolized the potential to create life. I would remain thankful for even the aches and pains that arrived monthly. Anything and everything related to creating, growing, and delivering a baby became holy to me. Every component was valued even more and considered a precious gift.

At my very core, I remained a mother. And permanently rooted in that core stemmed two main longings. The easiest to recognize was my longing to mother a future baby. I understood that need. It made sense. I looked forward to that day. But there was a second longing that I didn't fully recognize or understand. This equally strong, equally important longing was actually more of an instinct—to continue to mother my heaven baby. This primal response went deep. Initially, I couldn't identify this ongoing "itch." Wasn't it impossible to mother a baby who wasn't physically with me? Yet I wanted to do exactly that. But after I realized that this desire, this instinct, was a part of me, I was able to explore it, process it, live in it. The moment life was created inside of me, an unbreakable connection was also created.

My baby and I would always remain a part of each another. There is a permanent and unique bond that pushes into eternity. It doesn't matter that we are on different sides of heaven. We are connected.

One of the ways I have learned to mother my heaven babies is simply to share my story and talk about my babies' lives. Letting others enter into the continuing dialogue of my journey has given breath to memories of my heaven babies, and it constantly reminds me that they were real—real lives, real babies—and that I will forever be their mother. Another way I mother them is allowing myself to feel waves of sorrow. To sit down with my quilt and cry. To run my fingers across my hospital bands or read a sympathy note that was given to us. I mother them by celebrating them and thinking of them. I mother them by speaking of their lives. I mother them by participating in national days of remembrance when I, alongside thousands of other loss-mommas, light candles of remembrance. I also volunteer at the hospital that took care of my husband and me during the most difficult situation of our lives. I now get to walk into that building carrying hope, eager to share it with others who walk through those same doors as broken people.

I'm continually blessed by the lives of my heaven babies and remain connected to them in beautiful ways. Their lives continue to transform me by revealing profound truths about the goodness and love of God and about my identity in him. I have been able to experience a new depth with my Savior, and I am more acquainted with elements of his character that I was unaware of before. What an eternal gift.

After my first period, we started actively trying to get pregnant again. Sex had changed for me after our loss. Its purpose shifted from being an expression of love and connection with my husband to being more about getting pregnant. It was the physical act of making a baby. And I was very focused on sex because I was very focused on making a baby. I meticulously charted my cycle using ovulation strips and recording the progress and results. Since I didn't want to miss any moment in which I could potentially get pregnant, I'm pretty sure the week I knew I was ovulating became the best week of my husband's life. However, I understand this is not the case for every couple trying to get pregnant after a loss. Some relationships suffer as a result of trying so much every single month. The intense focus on baby-making isn't always relaxed or enjoyable, and has the ability to become a real strain on a relationship.

I very impatiently survived the "two-week wait." Like with my first pregnancy, I was feeling similar pinching sensations in my pelvic area along with tender breasts, which was exciting and scary at the same time. I was cautiously confident that I was pregnant and decided to take a pregnancy test. Taking a pregnancy test this time, compared to my first pregnancy, was completely different. The first time, I was simply focused on seeing those double lines. But this time, my mind carried the memories of my loss along with the hope of another baby. I longed to see those two lines, but I hesitated a little bit because I knew if I were pregnant, this pregnancy would be very different emotionally. And that brought on an entirely different set of fears and unknowns. But despite all the worries, I was eager and excited to know for sure. And sure enough, all of my husband's hard work and dedication paid off, and once again, we were staring at those two positive lines. I was filled to the brim with every emotion I could possibly feel—anxiety, excitement, fear, hope. We decided to wait a few days to share the news with anyone. We used that time to pray, focus, and steady our hearts. It was a special time for just my husband and me to know I was pregnant. No matter what happened with this pregnancy, we fiercely loved this baby already. This child was ours. I knew we would soon announce my pregnancy at least to our family. My heart needed somehow to include our heaven baby in the way we made the announcement, so I used those private, precious days to write a poem from the perspective of our heaven baby. I framed it and pinned a piece of my crocheted hospital quilt to the top of the page, right above the poem. It was a special way to include our heaven baby and celebrate the life growing inside of me—a way to connect them both. It was also a special keepsake that our families could tangibly hold as they, too, were still grieving our loss. The poem read,

You never got to see my face or tickle all my toes.
My hands were never held in yours, never kissed my little nose.
But so much love we already share and as I rest in Jesus's embrace
I'll be watching you from heaven until we get to see each other's face!
One day we will hug each other, this I know is true.
But until then, I'll hug you through my sibling,
August, two thousand twelve, is when he/she is due!
Love forever,
Baby Butler

Once I knew I was for sure pregnant and that we were going to share the news with family, a lot of fear dissolved and a naive confidence appeared. Or perhaps it was deliberate denial that another loss could happen. I was battling anxiety almost every day because the recent trauma of my first loss was still so fresh. I was still processing and grieving. There were constant whispers of doubt in my heart about this new pregnancy . . . *What if it happens again?* But I let the doctor's statements bounce off the walls in my brain: "Having a miscarriage, especially when it's the first pregnancy, is very common. From a doctor's standpoint, we aren't concerned after one loss. Many women go on to have healthy babies with no more losses." Multiple women I knew told me that they too had lost their first baby but went on to have two, three, even four healthy babies in a row. So I would rationalize and try to convince myself that this pregnancy would be healthy. *See? Women have healthy pregnancies after loss. Even medically, there's no reason to be concerned. It will be okay. It will be okay . . . it will be okay.* There were some days that I had to make a conscious effort to remember to lean into God, not the words of a doctor—that it was his promises that were unshakeable even when circumstances changed.

Nine months later and after an infinite amount of prayers and "it will be okays," I held my beautiful, healthy daughter. She was here. Safe. Healthy. Perfect. I didn't take a single moment for granted, because I knew things could have been different. I had not been exempt from the possibility of losing another baby or not being able to get pregnant in the first place. So my heart savored the sweetness of this joy because it knew all too well the bitterness of loss.

My arms had experienced the heaviness of emptiness, but now they knew the heaviness of fullness. And in some ways, I was thankful to know the heaviness of both—because both proved the steadfastness of my God. Empty or full, grief or joy, the power of Jesus was present and working—and good. Having a healthy baby was life-changing and beautiful. I was so thankful for a healthy pregnancy that led to holding a healthy child. But my baby wasn't a solution. She didn't fix the loss or grief of my first baby. I still needed Jesus. I needed him every day to hold my heart and direct my path that was covered with grief as well as joy. I had personally experienced his faithfulness and love despite either my emotions or my circumstances. It went deeper than that. He went deeper.

Amy's Story

I have a dear friend who was pregnant at the same time as I was. She was a few months further along, but we had been so excited to be pregnant together. After I lost my baby, she was so thoughtful in giving me the freedom to feel what I needed to feel. I wasn't jealous of her, but another dynamic of loss for me was that we wouldn't get to do it together. I was jealous of several other friends who were getting to share the experience with her. At her baby shower (which she expressly called and told me she would love to have me there but didn't want me to feel obligated to come and that if it was too hard to be there, she understood), I fought tears several times. When she asked me how I was doing, I told her I was rejoicing and grieving at the same time. I remembered Ezra 3:13, that after the temple had been rebuilt, there were mixed feelings about it in the crowd. The verse says no one could distinguish the sounds of joy from the sounds of weeping. I think my heart was a lot like that. I was so happy for her. And for several others who were pregnant. And I was hurting. And it was completely normal for both to live in my heart at the same time.

The first time we had sex after we miscarried, I sobbed the whole time. And he was so wonderfully tender with me. I had never experienced sex through the lens of grief. Through the lens of joy, laughter, tension, stress, silliness, forgiveness, anger, exhaustion—yes. Grief, no. It was healing for me to be close to him. I did worry about getting pregnant after my loss. And I think it changed how I experience pregnancy, especially early pregnancy. As I write this, I am pregnant with a little girl. At our first appointment, we found out our insurance only pays for one sonogram and that we would not be seeing the baby that day. I cried. And then we paid for an ultrasound out of pocket. I'm not sure I would need to see if we had not walked through miscarriage. Perhaps I would, but we'll never know. Since my first pregnancy led to a loss all other pregnancies have changed. I trust God. I know he has a plan. But I still wanted the ultrasound.

Erin's Story

Sex changed for me emotionally after losing our baby. It wasn't positive. My husband and I began to have a lot of problems associated with the loss of our baby, sex being one of them. It took me a long time to get to the point of enjoying sex again. I was just really hurting and so emotional, and it took a toll on me physically as well. I can say, thankfully, that this stage doesn't last forever. Sex can be amazing again!

For us, "trying again" meant IVF (in vitro fertilization) because the day we lost our daughter, I also lost my ability to have any more children without the help of IVF. We prayed about it and took a lot of time to think about IVF. We had our various thoughts about it, but in the end we knew the what-ifs for us would always be there if we didn't give it one try. So we decided to do just one round, no matter the outcome. Since adoption was already on our hearts, we felt God would give us our answer through that one try with IVF. We trusted in the Lord, and we knew he would stay faithful. It was hard to let go of that fear that it wouldn't work. I don't think I ever really did let go of that fear until years down the road.

I definitely worried about being able to get pregnant. Like I said, it was hard to let go of the fear that we wouldn't get pregnant again. It was terrifying to think we were literally "putting all our eggs into one basket" with our one try with IVF. I was scared to think that after all the physical pain, intramuscular shots, medicines, injections, surgery, hormones, thousands of dollars, time, and effort that we put into this one round of IVF, in the end it might not work. It was incredibly worrisome and hard to deal with the possibility of God denying us a baby we felt we so deeply wanted.

God's Promise

Blessed is she who has believed that
the Lord would fulfill his promises to her!
Luke 1:45 (NIV)

A Prayer

Father God,

From the moment I conceived my baby, he or she made me a mother. I will forever have that connection and be a mother to my child. Nothing can change that. My arms are heavy, Lord. They are heavy for the baby that now resides with you in heaven, and they are heavy for the future child I long to hold. I have a deep yearning and desire to mother a baby in my arms. I know the work of a mother is a special and sacred work. And Lord, every fiber of my being longs for that assignment. Please steady my heart, steady my feet, as I walk in faith and as you direct my path of motherhood—whatever that path looks like. In Jesus's holy name, amen.

Journal

You will always be the mother of your heaven baby—nothing will ever replace his or her life or the love you have for him or her. Moving forward does not mean forgetting. The deep longing to hold a baby in your arms and to raise a child is a beautiful calling. This longing has been placed inside of you by God, and he has not forgotten.

"May God himself, the God who makes everything holy and whole, make you holy and whole, put you together—spirit, soul, and body—and keep you fit for the coming of our Master, Jesus Christ. The One who called you is completely dependable. If he said it, he'll do it!" (1 Thess. 5:23–24 MSG).

Lean into God's word as he directs your steps. His plans for you are good. His love for you is strong. He fully understands the extent of your longing, and he will remain faithful.

What is the deep desire of motherhood speaking to your heart? What emotions come along with that calling? Anxiety? Guilt? Excitement? How can you continue to "mother" your heaven baby as you move forward on your future mothering journey?

CHAPTER SIX

again

Those we love and lose are always
connected by heartstrings into infinity.
—Terri Guillemets

When my daughter was a little over a year old, Christmastime had arrived and I became emotionally unstable overnight. One afternoon I began crying about . . . our Christmas tree. Not just crying, but desperately sobbing. Upon my request, we ventured out as a family to a tree nursery to choose our Christmas tree. We brought it home and got it set up in its base. A couple days later, my dear husband walked by the tree and casually said, "Hey cool. Look at all those little pinecones." I looked up . . . and lost it. Completely lost it. He rushed over to me and asked, "Are you okay? What's wrong? What happened?"

I tried to form the words clearly in my breathy response.

"Those . . . pinecones. They will never . . . grow bigger. Because . . . the tree is dead! It was cut down. And now it's dead and we bought it . . . and those baby pinecones . . . will never grow any bigger!" A sense of guilt and frustration washed over me. How in the world could I have let this happen? I'm the one who rescues stranded earthworms off the sidewalk after a rainstorm and returns them to the grass! I'm the one who heroically wrangles birds with broken wings and drives them an hour away to a bird rehabilitation center! I'm the one who loads up muddy dogs in my car at a busy intersection to bring them to our house until we find the owners! Well, technically I loaded muddy dogs in my brother-in-law's car (sorry, Bruce). And technically, it was to my mother- and father-in-law's house (sorry, parents). But the point is, I save! I rescue! I don't cut down and kill baby pinecones!

After I calmed down from my epic, hysteric pinecone breakdown, my husband lovingly (and bravely) suggested, "So . . . um . . . maybe we should take a pregnancy test. Just . . . to see." (I admired how he slipped the word *we* into that suggestion like we *both* would be peeing on a stick—like we *both* were crying about baby pinecones. Bless his heart.) I decided a pregnancy test was probably a good idea. Something was going on. I just wasn't myself. So I marched upstairs to see if peeing on a stick would give any clarity to my newfound passion for baby pinecones. And sure enough, double lines. Christmas had come early—I was pregnant! We were absolutely thrilled. Surprised, but thrilled. And I was extremely glad that my crazy was indeed pregnant-crazy, not regular-crazy that had suddenly taken control of my entire being. There is a difference.

I couldn't believe it. After I did the calculations, it was very possible that our daughter and this baby could share a birthday. Next Christmas we would be a family of *four*. The fact that this precious one was a surprise reassured me for some reason. I stayed hopeful, calmly optimistic. This baby was supposed to be a part of our family. I just knew it.

But because I had experienced the pain of losing a baby before, it had become second nature to hold my breath every time I went to the restroom. It was like this subconscious habit had formed and become a part of my daily routine. Each bathroom visit brought a moment of anxiety until I could see that the toilet paper was white and didn't display any signs of red. Then once I saw everything was normal, I could breathe again.

One morning as my husband and I were waiting for my mom to visit, I decided to go upstairs to get ready for the day. She was driving from a couple hours away to stay with us for Christmas. I was thrilled that she was going to be able to savor each sweet moment with us. I headed to the bathroom and held my breath like every time, wiped, and looked down. But this time was different. I felt like I had been punched in the heart—there was blood. My heart began to pound out of my chest. My hands shook. *Jesus, please no. Please, please, no.*

As I walked down the stairs to find Jarred, I began shaking so badly that it felt like the ground and walls were vibrating. I held on tightly to the railing of the staircase. "Jarred, I just wiped . . . and there's blood. There's blood." His face was covered in disbelief. "Okay . . . Are you hurting? Are you cramping?" At first I wasn't hurting, which allowed room for hope. But the cramping began only minutes later. The physical pain of our first loss was the only thing I had to compare to what my body was now experiencing. And since that loss had been so physically excruciating, I told Jarred, "Maybe it's something else. I just need to sit and hold still. I'm not in intolerable pain, so maybe . . . maybe everything's okay."

I called my OB's office. Since the office was closed because of Christmastime, I was transferred to the on-call doctor. The unfamiliar voice made me nervous. I wanted the familiar. I wanted something recognizable. The doctor informed me that because it was so early in this pregnancy—less than six weeks—they probably wouldn't be able to see a heartbeat. The only thing an ultrasound would show is whether or not the baby was there. She asked me how heavy I was bleeding and what my pain level was. She also informed me to watch for big clots. I hadn't passed anything substantial. Just silky blood. I asked some questions, processed her answers, and decided to sit and just . . . wait.

And that's exactly what I did. I sat back with my legs up on the ottoman, hoping. Hoping that if I could just hold still enough, the bleeding would stop and life would stay inside of me. However, my spirit did everything except hold still. I was in constant communication with God. Praying, praying, praying that everything would be okay, that this would be a miracle story. I told God that if he spared this child, I would tell everyone of what he had done. I pleaded. I begged. I rationalized. There was a constant battle in my mind. I have never been in a situation where waiting without answers tore so violently at my heart and mind.

To say that time stood still would be an accurate description of my day. I felt like every minute dragged along abnormally and painfully slowly. By far, it was the longest day of my life. I periodically texted my closest of friends. They kept checking in on me, telling me they were praying for baby. I knew they were—I felt every prayer. My precious friend and mentor, who has walked alongside me during many different seasons of my life, consistently texted me throughout the day with encouragement, even sharing her list of favorite chick-flick Christmas movies for me to watch to pass the time. That meant the world to me. Not only was she praying for me, but she also understood the weight of each passing second and how it added to my aching heart, so she helped distract me. And distraction was exactly what I needed. It was a practical act of love, and it soothed the sting a little.

I was being strangled by uncertainty. I don't know how else to describe it. I was just one tangled ball of emotions. I sat wearily, unsure of where I should let my heart fall. Hope? Or logic? Every time I tried to stay hopeful that our baby was alive, it was accompanied by the deep, painful awareness that our baby might not be alive. It was the first time in my life that trying to stay hopeful actually hurt. No matter how hard I tried to give in to hope, I couldn't fully release my heart. Because deep, deep down, I knew something was wrong. I had lost before. I wasn't naive to the fact that loss could happen again. I tried to keep a firm grasp on the trace amount of hope I had left, but it was like trying to hold a pile of sand. Every time I tightened my grip, more tiny grains of hope kept slipping away. My reality was, I was bleeding. Again. And it wasn't stopping; it was increasing. And I was cramping. The circumstance was full of unknowns, and I desperately longed for an answer. Any answer, as long as it was definite. The constant ebb and flow began to take a toll on me. And to be honest, the next couple of days were a complete blur. I have no distinct moments or memories. Just one long smudge of crying and hurting and praying.

As I rocked my daughter to sleep, I took refuge in those moments of quiet and peace, slowly swaying back and forth and back and forth in the darkness. It didn't take long before the rocking rhythm lulled her to sleep—her every muscle completely relaxed and her breathing became soft and tranquil. I quietly snuck out of her room. *Back to reality.* My daughter had been the only reason I was able to hold myself together. The urgency of taking care of her physically and emotionally didn't wane even in the hardest moments of my own pain. She is the kind of child who watches. She watches the people around her, especially Mommy and Daddy, and she absorbs the emotions. She's a sensitive and nurturing soul, far more than most adults I know. I wanted to protect her from the intense reality as best I could. I longed to keep Christmastime beautiful for her little one-year-old mind. But as hard as I tried to preserve her normalcy, I knew she was picking up on new emotions. Her sweet expressions and tender, intentional cuddles were proof that she knew something was going on. But oh, those cuddles were life-giving—completely life-giving.

The next night, I sat on the toilet, cramping. And just like that, a rush of blood poured out carrying with it a lot of tissue. I knew the life that been inside of me was no longer there. I walked halfway down the staircase to where the wall ended. I looked down into the living room to tell my husband and my mom that I was sure I had passed the baby. In a split second, all of the unknown, all of the fear, all of the sadness, all of the brokenness—all of it turned into rage. This felt like a very personal attack from the enemy. I balled up my fist and began punching the stairs over and over as hard as I could. My mom and husband rushed over and wrapped themselves around me. I was not angry with God. I was not angry with myself. I was angry because this attack felt very personal and intentional. I was angry at the enemy. I was angry that he thought this could be used to pull my heart away from my God. I was angry that

I would not know this baby here on earth. My angry physical outburst on the staircase woke my daughter, and we heard her little cries from her bedroom. Poor thing. What a way to wake up. My husband brought her down to the living room, and I nursed her and cuddled with her on the couch. The Lord knew that was exactly what I needed. Stillness. Calm. That connection between a momma and her baby. I ran my fingers through her soft blonde hair as she nursed and fell back to sleep. "I'm sorry, sweet girl," I whispered to her. As bad as I felt to have woken her up, I was once again thankful to cuddle with her that evening—just so I could hold her. Or so she could hold me. I didn't have a child to hold after I lost my first baby, so I knew the beauty and treasure I held in my arms this time. After she was relaxed, we laid her back down.

My husband retrieved everything out of the toilet. He collected it all in a glass. That was a definitive moment for me. I was walking through the darkness again.

I finally couldn't take it anymore. The physical pain had increased, although still not as bad as during my first loss. But the constant uncertainty made up for that. Even though I was almost positive that I had lost the baby, there was that continuous, painful thought of "what if"; that constant reminder of the many stories I had read online of bleeding occurring but the babies ending up completely healthy—where the substance passed was actually just clots, not the baby. What if I was one of those stories? What if my baby was one of those miracles? What if? I needed an answer, some form of clarity amid the foggy unknowns. I had to call the doctor again. I had to know for sure—no matter the outcome. It was Christmas Eve, so my OB's office was closed and once again I was connected to an unfamiliar voice. This one wasn't as warm as the one before. Her attitude was very matter-of-fact, like I was an annoyance for wanting an appointment since it was very obvious what was happening to me. Not exactly comforting. Already in a state of emotional breakdown, I used every ounce of restraint I could muster not to start sobbing or cursing right into my phone. "I know you won't be able to give me all the answers. But I need this. I have to know for sure. I can't take it anymore . . . just waiting." She paused for a moment, her firm voice softening a little. "I understand. You'll need to head to the ER then."

I was relieved that I would soon have a definitive answer. My momma watched our daughter at home as we headed to the ER. Even in the middle of chaos and pain, it was a huge emotional comfort to me to know that my daughter was with my mom. Oh, the comfort and love only a mother can bring. An irreplaceable, indescribable love that takes on human form in the shape of a momma. Knowing our daughter was having a fun day playing games and enjoying time with Grandma allowed Jarred and me to focus on each other and what was next.

Jarred and I walked up to the same large sliding glass doors that opened up into the same hospital I was in when I lost my first baby. I signed in at the same counter. I sat on the same side of the same waiting room. And then . . . they said my name. I stood up and walked towards the swinging doors that led to the actual ER. I was in pain but able to walk on my own, unlike my last visit down these halls. As the nurse guided us to the room I was assigned to, we passed by the very room where I felt God's sweet presence two years prior. That white-walled room that held my cries to Jesus, our prayers to our God, and the realization we would not be bringing home our baby. That sacred room where eternity and earth met—where heaven's kiss comforted earthly sobs. Oh, that blessed room.

The nurse directed us to a room not much farther down the hall. Bleeding heavily for that long was so uncomfortable. I just wanted to stand in a hot shower for hours. My muscles and my emotions craved it. Tests were done. Blood was drawn. Ultrasounds were taken. And then the nurse asked me to give a urine sample. My husband walked with me to the restroom where I attempted to pee in a cup without having blood also pour into it. I tried to clean up as best as I could and then returned to my bed. My nurse was a kind man. He was probably in his early fifties and had a short gray beard. The way he spoke and conducted himself was fatherly. I apologized for my urine sample being so filled with blood. "Oh, that doesn't matter at all," he reassured me. His compassionate smile and eyes relaxed my anxious heart. He looked over my chart. Then he looked up from his clipboard and smiled.

"You're my daughter's age." I smiled back and said, "That's so neat." His observation about my age was interesting to me. He was a daddy. His baby girl was my age. I wondered if the comparison stung his heart at all. I feel like it may have. I was hooked up to IVs, bleeding because I possibly—most likely—had lost my baby. Did he imagine his daughter in my same situation? Maybe she had been. I don't know for sure what he thought. But I know his comment made an impression on me. That seemingly small detail felt like a gift.

After what seemed like forever, the doctor came in and read over the results. It was confirmed: I had lost my baby. The doctor's attention was totally focused on us even though the hallways were busy and nurses kept popping in and out of our room. She clutched her clipboard full of paperwork at her chest and sat down. She was very sympathetic. The thing that stuck with me the most was how careful and gentle her terms and words were about my loss. I never felt like my pain was invalid because I was *just* five weeks along. She told me a chaplain would come in and talk with us, and shortly after, a lady walked in. I told her we had the baby in a glass and wanted the same thing we did for our first baby so that they could be together— ashes spread at the same remembrance bench along with other heaven babies.

My heart ached. So deeply. But this time, I called upon memory after memory of God's faithfulness through my first loss. The details were covered with his fingerprints. He was there. He mourned with us. I claimed his faithfulness once again. I clung tightly to him once again. I entrusted my broken heart to him once again. Because I knew it was only in his hands that my shattered heart could rest and be restored.

I knew he remained faithful.

Anneke's Story

I have had four miscarriages. The first was at six weeks, the second was at eleven weeks, the third was literally right after I told my husband we had a positive test, and the last one was again at six weeks.

I experienced physical pain with every miscarriage except for the third one because it was so early. In my first and fourth loss, I had a lot of heavy bleeding and cramping. My second was the worst, due to having a D&C and requiring a lot of healing time.

My first two were very hard on me. They were back-to-back, after months of trying and hoping every month. The second one we lost was the most difficult. I had no idea we had even lost the baby and found out during a routine appointment. I remember, when I got back to my car, I wailed and screamed the loudest and longest I ever had in my whole life. I was so angry and heartbroken. It took me a very long time to work through that.

By the time my third and fourth miscarriages happened, we had four children. I don't think I ever got emotionally attached to the third baby we lost, because I literally bled right after I found out and told my husband. It was bewildering and strange but not heartbreaking for me. When we lost our fourth, I was at a place where although it was very painful emotionally and I did not want to go down that road again, I found myself able to trust God with it completely and remain unshaken. For me it was an amazing transformation to see what God had accomplished in my heart over the years. I felt amazed at the grace I experienced in not wanting to recoil from him in anger, but instead wanting to cling to him tighter and plead with him not to let me go during it.

I named our first two Darcy and Delancy. I felt they had been girls. I didn't feel one way or the other for the last two, and I didn't want to name them generic names. I hope that I can still have the opportunity to give them names when I see them in heaven.

Keri's Story

I started having horrible pains in my lower abdomen. As I was nursing my nine-month-old, the pain got so bad that I had to put him down and run to the bathroom to take a bath—just to get some kind of relief. The pain finally went away, but the next day it started coming back. I called the nurse advice line, and I was told that if the pain occurred for four continuous hours, then I could go to the ER. My husband wasn't happy with that advice, so he went straight to the doctor on his military base and asked to speak with an ob-gyn. The doctor told him to take me straight to the emergency room. So we loaded up our son in the car and went to the closest ER. Once we arrived, they asked if I was pregnant and I told them I was not. They took a urine sample and blood sample from me—then they came back in and told me I actually was pregnant! I was so excited, and my husband was in shock! I was wheeled off to another room where an ultrasound could be done, but once they started looking, they could not find the sac. They thought it was just too early in the pregnancy to see everything and asked us to come back two days later to ensure my hormone levels were doubling. And they were doubling! I had some light bleeding in between ER visits, but I thought it was related to the vaginal ultrasound. My body felt fine, and I actually started to feel nauseous here and there.

About a week later, I started bleeding and became really scared and anxious. But I did not bleed in the volumes that I had when I had my first miscarriage, so I was hopeful. Because I was only six weeks along and my OB didn't want to see me that early, we went to the ER twice in one week. At the last ER visit, the doctor said my hormones had slightly dipped, which wasn't a good sign. She also said she could not locate the pregnancy, so she called our OB and said we absolutely had to be seen the following day. We were desperately asking God for a miracle. We met with my OB, and he said, looking at the ER report, that he was afraid it was ectopic but could not confirm anything until he performed an ultrasound. During the ultrasound he could not find the baby in my uterus or fallopian tubes. At that point he said he would need to do a D&C the next day. At six a.m. the following morning, I showed up for my procedure. I remember feeling sad when they used the term "abortion" instead of "miscarriage," but overall the staff was very sensitive to me. I was very heartbroken. Even though this baby was a surprise, my heart had already fallen in love! During the procedure they still couldn't locate the pregnancy. They had to put a camera down inside of me and eventually found the baby hanging in my abdomen. After waking up from the procedure, I remember feeling so thankful that the baby was not in the fallopian tubes because they did not have to remove any tubes. I was also thankful to be able to nurse my nine-month-old just twelve hours later, which was healing to my heart.

I had sensed that the Lord was speaking Psalm 118:17 to me—"I will not die but live, and will proclaim what the LORD has done" (NIV)—so it was very difficult for me when I lost that sweet baby. However, I believe the Holy Spirit showed me that that verse was actually for me and my womb. Had I not been seen when I was, it could have been extremely dangerous.

For each of my babies I have assigned a symbol. My first heaven baby is my Bear Cub. When we had my son, Noah, I gave him the symbol of an Arrow. And this third baby is my Feather Baby. "He will cover you with his feathers, and under his wings you will find refuge; his faithfulness will be your shield and rampart" (Ps. 91:4 NIV). I take great comfort knowing that Jesus is covering my baby with his feathers!

On August 31, a few weeks after my procedure, I woke up in the middle of the night with the happiest dream. In the dream I was lying on a hospital bed totally at peace, not anxious. A nurse was using a Doppler on my belly, and there was a strong heartbeat. She said I was four months pregnant. That was the entire dream, but I feel so strongly that it was the Lord encouraging me that he had another baby for me.

Getting back into a routine and chasing after my son made it really hard to find time to grieve. But one day when my son was napping, I saw a commercial that made me feel like it was time to grieve. The commercial was a trailer for a movie about a dad who loses his daughter. I turned off the TV and finally "went there." I wept and wrote letters to both of my heaven babies. This loss was about three months ago, and the grief still comes in waves. But I do not doubt the Lord's goodness and faithfulness to me. I know I will see the goodness of the Lord in the land of the living.

God's Promise

Just as you cannot understand the path of the wind or the mystery of a tiny baby growing in its mother's womb, so you cannot understand the activity of God, who does all things.
Ecclesiastes 11:5 (NLT)

A Prayer

My God,

After losing my first baby, I felt like the pieces of my heart would remain shattered forever. But, Jesus, I saw your goodness and I kept moving. I experienced life inside me again, and I fell in love with this child. But my heart is left trembling as I've lost a baby once more. The future and dreams I longed to share with this child are also lost. And the hope, which I desperately grasped onto, that I would know this child, is gone. This territory looks familiar yet feels so foreign and lonely. I need you now more than ever to draw me closer to you. My heart and mind need supernatural guarding. Infuse every molecule of my body with your breath of life. Cover my every thought with your steadfast love. Calm the storms of anxiety with your promises. Remind me, Jesus, of the faithfulness you showed me before so that I may walk in confidence that you will remain faithful to me now. In your holy and faithful name, amen.

Journal

Maybe your heart has recoiled from God after loss happened again. Or maybe your heart has fallen deeper into his heart, desperately seeking his comfort. Either way, God is present in the details of this loss and he isn't afraid of or offended by your questions and emotions. He wants to walk alongside you now just as he did before. When another loss happens, recalling the goodness of God that you experienced in your previous loss will transform you. Thanking God for his faithfulness in the past will stabilize your heart in the present.

"Let all that I am praise the LORD; may I never forget the good things he does for me" (Ps. 103:2 NLT).

How was God faithful to you during a previous loss or previous losses? Write down the acts of God's goodness and faithfulness that you experienced in the past. What truth from before can you claim and apply now as you walk through new loss and grief?

CHAPTER SEVEN

remember

A human life is a story told by God.
—Hans Christian Andersen

After my first loss, my heart became focused on one thing: finding an ornament for our Christmas tree. But not just any ornament, *the* ornament that would represent our baby during the holidays. One that would remind us of God's goodness and faithfulness through our loss. One that would tangibly tie our baby's life into all future Christmases. Something I could carefully unwrap with my future children and explain to them the importance of that ornament. Something that would remind others of my baby. Because even at Christmas, a lighthearted time filled with cheer, I still wanted to talk about my baby. I always wanted to remember and celebrate the life waiting for me on that side of heaven. So the search for my ornament began. I wanted something simple and delicate. My heart knew what the ornament looked like, even when my mind couldn't envision it. The moment I saw it, I would just know.

I told no one of my search. Only my husband and my God knew that the seemingly minor object that I longed to hang on our tree was profoundly important to me. It was only October but stores already had their aisles overflowing with Christmas decor. I normally would have complained about how far in advance stores wanted to sell things or how Thanksgiving felt skipped over, but not this time. I was happy to be able to start my blessed search. Being able to take action and look for something to symbolize my baby kept everything feeling real—feeling close. Shiny bulbs, sparkly lights, and jolly Santa figurines filled the shelves from top to bottom. The twinkling Christmas tree display provided a lovely atmosphere for the sorrowful reason I roamed the aisles. Shopping carts were filled with red and green. A couple little children walked with their parents, taking in the flickering lights and the bright and gleaming objects, their faces covered in nothing but excitement and eagerness for the fun that Christmastime was sure to bring them. Sweet, precious innocence. I smiled at the family as they walked by, praying they would only ever know beauty at Christmastime.

As I walked the holiday section of that first store, I felt confident the search for my ornament would be fairly simple. I was always overwhelmed with the abundance of ornaments to choose from during the holidays. However, now that I was looking for a specific one, my search increased in difficulty. After searching every department, every shelf, every display, I still hadn't found one. And after the fifth and sixth stores, my hopeful spirit began to lessen. Each place provided memorial ornaments, but none of them were right. None of them triggered the response of recognition that I was anticipating.

It became my daily prayer that the Lord would lead me to the ornament. "Oh Father, I need my baby's ornament. Please lead me to it. To others this might seem unimportant, but to me it is everything. It's so important to me. And I know you care about the smallest of details in my life, so please lead me to my ornament."

Christmas quickly approached but there was still no memory ornament to hang on our tree. My heart ached. I refused to buy an ornament just for the sake of having an ornament. I needed *the* ornament.

And then, one afternoon, my husband walked into the apartment with a package in his hands from my "adopted" Aunt Anna. Aunt Anna is one of those rare women who infuses life into your spirit every time you talk. Since she and I are not blood related, I decided to take matters into my own hands and claim her as my own. I opened the unexpected package and peeked inside at its contents. I pulled out a small white box the size of my hand. My heart began to pound, and my tear-filled eyes couldn't believe what they were seeing. Oh, but my spirit recognized it completely. I held a white heart ornament with a pearly sheen. It had circular ripples like what happens when a small pebble hits the glassy surface of water. How fitting that visual was. A small teardrop pearl delicately dangled from the bottom—a gold charm clung to the ribbon on top that displayed the year, 2011.

Aunt Anna didn't know about my search. She didn't know how many stores I had scoured. She didn't know how deeply my heart ached for this ornament. My aunt mailed it to me, but my God sent it to me. And his specific care for me filled my heart. *I see you, sweet daughter. I hear you. I know how important this is to you. Here is your perfect ornament. I remain faithful. I am here.*

This ornament represented my heaven baby. But it also ended up representing the intimate care, miraculous power, and endless love of a Sovereign God for his daughter. And a strong, eternal truth was solidified in my heart that day—my God is a God of details. It would be something I looked back on for the rest of my life as a reminder of how good, how loving, how personal my Savior is.

Two years later, the Christmas season of 2013 had arrived, and we found out I was pregnant. This holiday season promised joy and sweet memories. But after spending Christmas Eve in the ER where it was confirmed I had miscarried at five weeks, three days, Christmastime looked absolutely nothing like we had anticipated. After the hospital released me, I could not wait to get home to my daughter and my mom. I also knew I would see our first heaven baby's ornament hanging on our Christmas tree. I told Jarred I wanted to stop by the mall to get an ornament for this baby. Since the following day was Christmas, I wanted our babies' ornaments to be close to each other.

As we exited off the highway and I saw the dense traffic and overflowing parking lots, my heart sank. I was far too physically and emotionally depleted to push my way through crowds of last-minute shoppers, so I decided to go straight home and rest.

We pulled up in our driveway, and I don't think I have ever experienced such an overwhelming sense of home before. There was a small box on our doorstep. As we made our way inside, I picked it up to see who had sent it. It was from Aunt Anna. I cut the tape that sealed the package and pulled out the bunched-up tissue paper.

I tried the best I could to steady my shaky voice and get the words out. "Jarred, come see this." I held up an ornament with an obvious and striking resemblance to our first heaven baby's ornament. Not only was it also a heart, but the pearly color and the ribbon were the exact same. The silver words written on the front pierced by heart. "Connected by love, Guided by faith."

Guided by faith. That truth had become the only direction I knew. It didn't mean blindly following someone. It meant making the decision to trust my faithful God through every step of my journey. It meant trusting that he worked for my good even when I couldn't see it or feel it. It meant believing he was bigger than what was happening. It simply meant walking with him, following him. Even when the steps felt unsteady. Even when the steps felt too big or too painful to take. I knew my God was faithful and that he was present in every detail of my life.

Aunt Anna didn't know that I had lost another baby. She didn't know that I had spent Christmas Eve in the ER. She mailed the box days before even I knew that I had lost the baby! But my God knew—because he is a God who sees. He saw my baby. He saw me. He knew the exact emergency room I would be in. He knew the exact hospital bed I would be lying in as I prayed to him and declared him faithful.

Almighty God was pouring out specific signs of his faithfulness and detailed acts of his love days before any person on this earth knew my baby had died. That is the God I will forever put my trust in and eternally give my life to.

Those Christmas ornaments from Aunt Anna have become the way I include our heaven babies into every Christmas season. I suppose I could keep them displayed somewhere year-round, but I find it healing to take them carefully out of their little boxes every year and intentionally display them for the season. There are other little evidences of my babies' lives all over my house. For everyday life, I display the crocheted mint-green shawl that I received the night I lost my first baby. It remains my most precious object of comfort. For the first few weeks after my loss, I slept with it every night. It gave my empty arms something to hold onto. It was something to wrap around my aching stomach. After a while, it stayed folded nicely on my bedroom dresser, easily seen and accessible if I needed to grab it. My precious sister painted a beautiful quilt rack that now hangs on my bedroom wall. One end is stamped with the words Baby Butler 2011. The top of the rack is a shelf and displays precious objects for both my heaven babies and incorporates their lives into our everyday lives. I often find myself picking up the objects, running my fingers over the silky green shawl, or brushing the soft yarn against my face.

In addition to everyday life and Christmastime, I look forward to including the memory of our heaven babies in other holidays, such as Mother's Day. My most treasured Mother's Day so far was in 2014. After church we headed over to my pastor's house for a Mother's Day lunch. Our attendance at their dinner table was an almost weekly occurrence for their epic "Sunday dinners." Our pastor, his wife, and their four children have played major roles in our lives. They have sat on the floor crying and grieving with us. They have embraced us and celebrated the sweet moments with us. They have showed us how to love well like Jesus. They have made Jarred and me better partners, better parents, and better people. This particular Sunday dinner was extra meaningful, though. All four of their children had also recently lost babies in miscarriages, so we all shared a sense of unity and grief. With it being Mother's Day, I felt extra fragile. I was so thankful to be sharing the day with them. They understood the wide range of emotions I was experiencing because they were also experiencing it all. I walked into their kitchen and saw a beautiful remembrance table set up. In the center of the large round table, a tall bouquet of bright yellow flowers stood overlooking each of the candles that lined the outside edge of the table. Next to every lit candle was a name card displaying each of our heaven babies' names or nicknames. It was a powerful visual and a comforting reminder that all of our babies were together. My daughter was almost two years old, and I was pregnant with her sister. There in that kitchen, I felt like all four of my babies were together. I stood quietly, soaking in the blessed atmosphere.

Connecting with other moms who have experienced losing babies connects our hearts in profound ways. That's one reason I look forward to October 15th every year. In 1988, Ronald Reagan designated the month of October as Pregnancy and Infant Loss Awareness Month, and on the 15th at seven p.m. local time, mommas from around the world light candles in remembrance of their babies. I light two candles. My husband and I sit together in the dark, our only source of light coming from the flickering candles. We take time just to focus and feel. Feel the heaviness. Feel the beauty. We talk about the details of the past and what is ahead in our future. We remember how far we've come on this journey. We also acknowledge that we are still on it—this lifelong journey of life after loss. There is something incredibly beautiful about doing the same thing at the same time as other grieving parents. There are so many different ways that we have chosen to celebrate and remember our babies. And each way brings a different part of my heart healing and joy—whether it's lighting a candle, displaying my shawl, hanging up my ornaments, or . . . getting tattooed.

For my thirty-first birthday, the celebration started a few days before my actual birthday (as it should, am I right?). I opened my first present, which was a new sketchbook and art kit lined with fresh pencils, pens, chalk, and other drawing supplies. My immediate reaction to this gift was giddiness. I had been telling Jarred for months that I wanted to start drawing on a consistent basis again, so I didn't read any deeper into that gift. But as I was looking through it all, he said, "I wanted to give this present to you a few days early. You're going to need a little time to sketch up some ideas for the memory tattoos we're getting together this weekend." I cried. And it wasn't the cute kind. It was the full-on ugly cry. We had wanted to get tattooed after our losses, so to think it would actually be happening was surreal. And for the next few days, I drew constantly. What a lovely mission.

Lavender had been such a special scent to us after we lost our first baby, so I knew I wanted to incorporate a lavender flower into my tattoo. The word "faithfulness" had been permanently imprinted on my heart. After a lot of thinking and praying (and Pinteresting), I decided on a lavender flower with the word "faithfulness" as the stem. It fully represented my loss, grief, healing, and hope, and it testified to God's faithfulness I had come to know intimately. I very (very) quickly sketched it and decided that that would be the inspiration sketch. I would take it to the tattoo artist so that he could recreate it more cleanly and professionally.

First thing the morning of my birthday, festivities began. We had a delicious breakfast, went to a movie, and then to lunch. Next was the most anticipated part of my day. We headed into the tattoo studio, and surprisingly I was the only one wearing a baby. I handed the artist my piece of doodled paper I had ripped out of my sketchbook. He went to the back room for a couple minutes. When he came back out, he had my drawing on the tattoo paper, ready to transfer onto my skin. "Oh, that was just a quick drawing I did. I was going to have you redraw it," I said. He replied, "Oh, okay. Well, I'd be happy to redraw it for you. But I think it looks really good." Since he was the professional, I had expected him to redraw it—to polish the rough edges, to make every little petal and letter and line perfect. But I thought through it for a moment and realized that this ordinary piece of torn paper was marked in the same way I was—imperfect, testifying to the faithfulness of God. So I told him, "You know what? Yeah. Let's do this one." My heart was permanently marked by my heaven babies' lives. My heart was permanently marked by the power of Jesus. And now my body would be permanently marked too. And God's faithfulness will always overwhelm my imperfections.

But he said to me, "My grace is sufficient for you, for my power is made perfect in weakness." Therefore I will boast all the more gladly of my weaknesses, so that the power of Christ may rest upon me.
2 Corinthians 12:9 (ESV)

I decided to have it placed on my left forearm where I would be able to see it every day. As I raised my hands in worship, held my babies, or used my arms to work, create, help—the reminder was there: God was faithful.

The artist began tattooing me. Within seconds, my skin was stunned by the odd combination of numbness from the vibrating tattoo gun along with the pain from the needles. The entire process of getting the tattoo felt so similar to my loss journey itself. The numbness. The pain. The blood. The gentle care I had to be intentional about for weeks after. And then, as the top layer of skin fell off and it began to heal, the tattoo was *beautiful*. I could see all the details that weren't visible before. The colors were brighter. The lines were stronger.

Proverbs 3:3 says, "Let not steadfast love and faithfulness forsake you; bind them around your neck; write them on the tablet of your heart" (ESV). Bound around my neck. Written on my heart. Now tattooed on my forearm. So very fitting that my body should permanently carry the mark too.

There have been many times that a new layer of grief emerges that I was previously unaware of. Something new inside of me stirs up, and I'm left in a tornado of emotions. And that's exactly what happened when I decided to give both of my heaven babies personal names.

After we lost our first baby, the name we immediately began using was Baby Butler. It happened naturally and unintentionally. Because we didn't know the gender, our baby didn't have an actual first name but held our last name—and Baby Butler just worked. That was the name I used, and it was the name others used. I didn't think any more about it.

However, when we lost our second baby, I was faced with a dilemma. The sympathy cards and texts and messages that we received all referred to Baby Butler. But to me, Baby Butler was our first baby. This loss was a separate loss. This baby was a separate baby. Baby Butler was not meant to be a default name that could be placed on them both. But I had no substitute name, so it kind of became just that—a label, not an actual name.

For a year, I prayed with a longing—a longing that almost hurt—to name my heaven babies. It became this big thing to me that I could not stop thinking about. I was not just naming past losses; I was giving names to my children who just happened to live in heaven.

I felt a constant sense of incompleteness. There were so many factors. What I knew was that I did not want to give our heaven babies gender-specific names. And I did not want names that simply sounded nice. It had to feel right. When I found them, I would just know, just like I had known my ornaments.

In her loss story, Keri (one of the other loss-mommas in this book), shares that her heaven babies as well as her earth baby are represented by different meaningful symbols—either from words that God has given to her or through special Bible verses. When I first read that, I thought that was so beautiful.

I didn't have words or symbols that I associated with my heaven babies. But I could immediately identify specific things that reminded me of each of our heaven babies—scents. For our first baby, it was undeniably the scent of lavender. One evening, my husband was sitting next to me, and we started talking about how sacred the smell of lavender was to us. That scent was so tied to my heart that I couldn't mindlessly spray or smell it without making sure my heart and mind were in a place to experience it. It took me back to that time of tenderness and rawness. We began having a sweet conversation about how every time we breathe that scent, our hearts and minds immediately think about our first baby. And in what felt like a divine moment of enlightenment, that word sounded new, like we had never heard it before—*lavender*.

Lavender.

That was it! How had I not seen it before? Our first baby's name had always been Lavender.

I began crying tears of peace and gratefulness and relief that our first baby had a name. We began to further reminisce. We shared memories of our second baby with each other. We had learned I was pregnant after Thanksgiving that year and lost the baby on Christmas Eve. The only reason I even took a pregnancy test was because of my complete and utter breakdown about baby pinecones. Needless to say, our Christmas tree played an important role during that time. On top of the humor that remembering that story brings to us, my husband reminded me how every molecule in our house smelled like pine that season. Our living room was small, so the moment you opened the front door, the smell of pine was wonderfully overwhelming. I always thought a Christmas or winter name was suitable for our second baby, but none of the typical Christmas names felt right. And then he suggested Pine.

Pine.

Both of their names flowed out of our mouths in one evening after a year of praying and longing. Oh Lord, thank you. They are perfect.

Naming my heaven babies has been one more connection I have with them. Being able to call them by their names brings a sense of wholeness to my spirit. It is such a healing gift. But more than anything, my strongest ongoing need is to continue to talk about them. As long as I'm talking about Lavender and Pine, their memories have breath.

To say the process of grieving is complicated would be a major understatement. There is no straight line to healing. In my own experience I've felt that my healing process is more of a spiral than a line. I have found myself many times spiraling back to familiar pains that I thought I had found peace with. And other times I've circled around new pains that I'm totally unfamiliar with. I'm constantly learning to embrace my changing, sometimes unpredictable spiral. Because sometimes it's in the times of circling back to the pain and the rawness of my losses that I feel the closest to them again. And sometimes new connections are made. For those reasons, I will happily flow in that spiral forever.

Keri's Story

There are different things that continue to bring me comfort and help me celebrate my babies' lives. After I lost my first baby, my sister made me a box with cards in it to write to my baby. It took a long time to sit down and write something, but I knew it was there for me whenever I was ready. God also gave me a picture of my first baby playing with my sisters' babies in heaven. I think about that picture often. I have two remembrance necklaces that I wear when my heart especially needs it. I will also ask God, "Please tell my babies hello and that daddy and I love them!"

Megan's Story

I love to get to talk about Eliana and to share my story with others. I try not to say "the miscarriage"; I call her by her name. It feels good and reminds me that Eliana is a real person—my daughter. And that brings me more healing.

On Eliana's due date, September 21, 2013, my friend gave me a beautiful wind chime with the words "Eliana, loved beyond words, and missed beyond measure" engraved on it. It blesses me every day and is a beautiful reminder of her. The sound of the chimes reminds me that she is real, and that God answered my prayer and healed her—even if her healing was attained by entering into heaven.

I have only talked about Eliana with my five-year-old since my other two are under three years old. Our wind chime is not only a special gift to me but also a tangible object that I've used with my five-year-old to talk about Eliana. It makes for an easy conversation starter when we talk about her. It's hard to explain death and heaven and eternity to a child so young, but

I try to explain to her that she has another little sister in heaven, and for a reason that we can't understand right now Jesus wanted her in heaven with him instead of here on earth with us. Even though Eliana never lived here on earth with us, she lives in our hearts, and I try to express that to my oldest daughter as best as I can by talking about her as a person and part of our family. She doesn't quite understand it all right now, but just knowing that she knows Eliana's name and that she is in heaven is a blessing to me. In her sweet five-year-old voice, she sometimes asks if we will ever be able to go visit Eliana.

As my three girls here on earth get older, we will continue to talk about their heaven sister. It's difficult right now just because they are so young and don't understand it all, but it won't stop me from talking about Eliana when the moment arises. I want them to know that Eliana is real and that she is as much a part of our family as they are.

God's Promise

I will remember the deeds of the LORD;
yes, I will remember your wonders of old.
I will ponder all your work,
and meditate on your mighty deeds.
Psalm 77:11–12 (ESV)

A Prayer

Father,

Thank you for the life of my baby. I celebrate the beautiful mark that my child has left on my life and in this world. As I remember my baby's life, I also remember that you are a faithful God. You walk with me through the darkness and carry me when I can no longer stand. You never leave me nor abandon me. Even when my circumstances are painful and don't make sense, I can live confidently in your care because I know you are a good Father who loves me. Thank you. In the name of Jesus, amen.

Journal

And Joshua set up at Gilgal the twelve stones they had taken out of the Jordan. He said to the Israelites, "In the future when your descendants ask their parents, 'What do these stones mean?' tell them, 'Israel crossed the Jordan on dry ground.' For the Lord your God dried up the Jordan before you until you had crossed over. The Lord your God did to the Jordan what he had done to the Red Sea when he dried it up before us until we had crossed over. He did this so that all the peoples of the earth might know that the hand of the Lord is powerful and so that you might always fear the Lord your God."

Joshua 4:20–24 (NIV)

God saved the Israelites by leading them through the Jordan River. He didn't direct them around the Jordan, and he didn't keep them at the edge of the waters. He provided a way straight through the Jordan by parting the waters. What looked like a seemingly impossible obstacle became the Israelites' divine pathway to life. God told Joshua to take the twelve stones that had been taken out of the Jordan and set them up so that the people, as well as future generations, would look to them and remember God's faithfulness and power and miracles in their lives.

As you have walked through your loss, what evidences of God's love for you have you experienced? What stones of remembrance can you set up in your own life as a memorial and reminder of God's faithfulness?

CHAPTER EIGHT

redeemed

I carried you every second of
your life, and I will love you for
every second of mine.
—Unknown

Whoever said that time heals all wounds obviously never lost a baby. Maybe time will heal physical wounds, but a deeply wounded heart—one that grieves the loss of a baby along with a lifetime's worth of love, hopes, and dreams? No, time cannot completely heal anything that precious and complex.

Time continues to pass by, but the ache from my losses remains. I still occasionally run my fingers over my mint-green shawl and cry fresh tears. I still find myself staring out the window remembering the details of the emergency room that I was in on Christmas Eve. Not only is remembering a normal part of the process, but it can also be healthy and healing. Forgetting the pain would be tragic because we would lose so much more than the pain itself. It is within the details of our losses and grief that we see the raw power, goodness, and love of Jesus for his sons and daughters. Remembrance is made up of holy, tear-soaked moments of grief and celebration, and I welcome each and every one of them. I welcome those moments because it brings me to that sacred atmosphere again—where heaven meets earth and the air exudes God's faithfulness in its most condensed form.

It can still be difficult sometimes to reconcile the reality of my suffering with the truth that God is all-powerful and good.

If God is in control, why didn't he stop my losses from happening?

Did God cause my losses?

Honestly, I don't know the answers or understand why I lost my babies. There are countless opinions and theories on the matter. And I'm not entirely sure where my theology is on the topic. It may never be settled. And as much as my flesh wants, even demands, answers, there will never be full satisfaction. How can a finite mind comprehend an infinite God?

But this is what I do know. I know that I felt the presence of the Holy Spirit more powerfully in an emergency room after I lost my baby than I have anywhere else . . . even at church. It wasn't within the confines of comfort but outside on the battlefield of brokenness that his presence was so tangible I felt I could reach out and grab him. In a single moment, losing my babies stripped away the superficial and insubstantial. It shook everything I knew, or thought I knew. Like the aftermath of a devastating earthquake in a small town, my heart was a pile of rubble. The structures I had built in my life were now destroyed, flattened. Through the dust and debris, the only thing left was Jesus. He remained—not as some distant entity, but as an intimate Savior standing with me in the middle of my ruins.

The greatest miracles have happened after great suffering. Isaiah 61:2–4 speaks of this incredible exchange of emptiness for fullness:

to proclaim the year of the LORD's favor,
and the day of vengeance of our God;
to ***comfort all who mourn;***
to grant to those who mourn in Zion—
to give them a ***beautiful headdress instead of ashes,***
the ***oil of gladness instead of mourning,***
the ***garment of praise instead of a faint spirit;***
that they may be called oaks of righteousness,
the planting of the LORD, that he may be glorified.
They shall ***build up the ancient ruins;***
they shall ***raise up the former devastations;***
they shall ***repair the ruined cities,***
the devastations of many generations. (ESV, emphasis added)

But before the comfort, the beauty, the gladness, and the restoration, there are ashes, mourning, a faint spirit, and destruction. The Israelites found freedom after crossing the Jordan River (Josh. 3), but the miraculous parting of the waters came after the suffering of being slaves for generations. The Son of God—our sinless, pure, holy Savior—was familiar with pain. The redemption of mankind came through the suffering and death of Christ himself on the cross (Matt. 27:27–44).

My heart has settled. Not in a place of answers or understanding, but in a place of trust. My desire to trust God slowly became stronger than my desire to know why. Eventually, I released the whys and exchanged them for intentional faith.

God has redeemed my losses. When I say he has *redeemed*, I don't mean *fixed*. I don't mean that everything is now okay or that my pain is gone. I am eternally grateful for the healing and truth I've experienced, but I'm not glad that my losses happened.

My losses have not been restored, but my heart has been. If left to my own devices, no good would have come out of it. There would be no redemption or healing. Through the power of Jesus and his love for me, I am redeemed. My losses are redeemed.

Every baby leaves a uniquely shaped void in a momma's heart, taking with them pieces that will remain missing until we are reunited again. Our incompleteness only makes sense, doesn't it? How can we feel completely whole when a part of us is gone? But it's those parts that Jesus will fill with his presence. Healing and even beauty are possible again. We can catch glimpses of eternity if only we'll look for them. We can see his fingerprints on the details of our lives.

And as life-changing and beautiful as that truth is, it is merely a taste of the beauty that awaits us on that side of heaven.

Amy's Story

God was so merciful to me in the midst of my loss. I think first and foremost, God gave himself. I believe the words of Jesus in Matthew 5:4 were most tangible to me in the waiting and in the loss itself. "Blessed are those who mourn, for they shall be comforted" (ESV). His word, his Spirit, his people, even some particular songs were God's arms wrapped around me in the suffering. His comfort is personal. His comfort is tangible. His comfort is practical. His comfort stays with you. It's powerful. It's tender. That would have been enough. By grace upon grace, I continue to see redemption in a variety of ways even to this day.

One of the sweetest things that God gave me in the midst of my grief was women who shared in my suffering. My heart is inextricably tied to several women who shared their own stories of miscarriage with me. Some who had lost before, some around the same time, and some much later—a precious sorority that no one would ever volunteer for, but that has a depth of relationship that is hard to replace.

He has also given me a greater depth of compassion for women who have miscarried and for grief in general. Experience is an excellent, albeit difficult, teacher. When someone I know miscarries, I am among the first to reach out, to wrap my arms around her, to cry with her, to bring a meal (as so many did for me). I will always have a tender place in my heart for the woman whose womb carried both life and death.

One way that God has redeemed the loss of my baby is with the most lovely thoughts of her. I will share a few. (1) The only part of this broken world she will ever experience is the comfort of my womb. Her first sights and sounds, tastes, smells will all be of heaven. The light that touches her face comes from the very presence of God. Death has no sting because the first hand she will hold is the hand of our Savior. (2) I like to think she will show me around when we get to heaven and do her best to catch me up on things my mind cannot even imagine in its most creative moments. (3) I have told several dear ones who have miscarried as well that I just know our babes are the best of friends. They care for each other well. We share grief in common. They got to skip the shadow and move straight to reality.

Perhaps these last two thoughts are merely sentimental. I have no biblical truth to make a compelling case for them. But they are lovely, aren't they?

Anneke's Story

I absolutely have seen God redeem my losses. Here is the beautiful thing about knowing God. When you face all these painful things on the earth with him by your side, the treasure of the outcome becomes as life-changing as the loss itself. I know that is a hard thing to swallow when you are going through something horrible. It is only during the depths of tragedy that we are forced and pressed to see God in new ways. We experience his companionship afresh, his compassion, his tears of sorrow as he bears our pain with us, his strength, his kingship, his whispers of encouragement, and his shoulders of comfort. If you've ever had a friend who was there with you when you couldn't face something on your own, you know how bonded you are to that person after the brunt of the tragedy is over. You've bonded in a way that never would have occurred without those hard circumstances, and you appreciate that person in a new way because you've seen a beautiful side of them that you hadn't known before. It's the same when you have a perfect, loving, eternal Father who carries you through the pain.

Keri's Story

I think redemption is recognizing God's heart in the matter. He allows these things to happen—but he works all for our good.

My husband and I prayed, fasted, and asked God when we should try to get pregnant. Both our hearts clearly heard "April." Sure enough, we got pregnant in April. Since my nickname is Bear, we named our baby Bear Cub. After we lost our little Bear Cub, we decided to spend some time away together. We drove up to Yosemite and then to Lake Tahoe. I thought it would be amazing to see a bear, so I prayed we would see one. As we drove along Lake Tahoe, we didn't see a bear . . . we saw a bear cub just playing right next to us! I felt like God was saying that our little Bear Cub was with him in heaven, and that he would grant us more bear cubs in the future. Seeing the bear cub was very redemptive for me. We also felt like God gave us a name of a future baby—a promise that we would have another child.

As I look back at our losses, I can definitely see God's hand in the details of those times. For our first baby, it was a miracle that we even got pregnant the month he said we would. It was meant to be! Even for how short the pregnancy was, it was still amazing! God's hand was there as he gave us promises and allowed us to see the bear cub. He is totally for us.

One thing I want to encourage other grieving mothers

to do is praise God through it all. Nothing about our losses will ever make sense, but God will work it for our good. If you don't walk through something yourself, how can you walk alongside others? I also recommend buying a piece of jewelry to symbolize the gift of that baby's life, no matter how brief. Give yourself grace. There are a ton of hormones that go on in our bodies after loss. I am a worship leader, and I completely lost it on stage singing about how our resurrected King has defeated the sting of death! I could not stop bawling in front of seven hundred people! I was so embarrassed. I looked out and saw my husband weeping too. It was brutal. But in the process, God allowed healing to erupt in that place for many people, not just myself! As awkward as it felt, it was actually a powerful and amazing thing. Give yourself the freedom to grieve. Be intentional about your grieving. It will come in waves.

Erin's Story

Redemption is really the theme of my husband's and my journey. God has shown his glory and faithfulness through the loss of our babies by blessing us with the miracle of adoption. God has taught us so much. I felt closest to him when we were going through the process of adopting our son.

In a way, you are never fully recovered in your loss. It still hurts, it is still painful, and you never "get over" the loss of a baby. But what you can see is God's redeeming love and grace through it all. My husband and I always talked about adoption. Even when we were dating, we would say, "How cool would it be to adopt one day?" What we didn't know was that it was a quiet seed God planted there early on in our relationship to prepare us because he knew that adoption would be part of our story. We were meant to be adoptive parents and have one biological child.

See, this is a two-part story for me. The first story of grace and redemption actually goes back to our biological child. When my husband and I were in college, we had known each other several years, but we had only been dating about three months when we found out we were pregnant. We were shocked. I didn't know what to do, but I knew one thing—I was keeping the baby. I was a senior in college, about to graduate with my bachelor's degree. I was a young, scared, unwed girl, whose parents were going to kill her. I knew deep down that this baby was special and meant to be here at this time for a very specific reason. My husband and I had known the Lord in our younger years but had been straying, and our lives turned upside down when we found out we were pregnant. Individually we decided to pursue a relationship with the Lord and get our lives back on track. We rededicated our lives to Christ, and that October a beautiful brown-eyed, curly-haired boy was born. Little did we know that our surprise baby would be our only biological child. We were married that following February. We had great plans to have another child. I always talked about doing this or that for my future pregnancy and labor.

Here's the cool part—the redemption part, the part that still amazes me: had it not been an unexpected, unplanned pregnancy, way earlier than we would have liked, we never would have had any biological children. Because just a few years after our son was born, I lost my ability to have any more. Had we waited, been engaged a year, married the following year, and then probably decided to keep waiting to try to get pregnant, it would have been too late. My ovary would have burst at that point. And not only would I have lost my ability to have biological children, but I also probably wouldn't be here. If it wasn't for our second pregnancy during the time my ovary had burst, I would have never known I was internally bleeding. I share all of this to say, God is redeeming. He knows what he is doing. There is a plan for everything! Even if we stray, even if we go off God's course for us, even if we experience tremendous loss, his timing is perfect. It may all make sense one day or it may not until heaven. My husband and I have made it through some tremendous loss and pain, and through it all, we remain together. That's God's redemption and love.

The second part of my story of God's redemption through our loss is when we lost our daughter and our future babies through our failed IVF attempt. We knew quite simply that God was not going to allow us to have any more biological children.

We were encouraged to try IVF again and again by our friends and family, but our hearts kept leading us back to adoption. It was never a backup plan for us. We just had to wait for the right timing to pursue it, and let me tell you, it was perfectly timed. I don't know why I'm always surprised with God's plan for things and how they align. Immediately after finding out our IVF round failed, that we were indeed not pregnant, I called my mom. She gave me some of the best advice she ever had. She said to me, "Erin, this all must have happened because there is a baby already born out there that you're meant to be the mother of." My mom ended up passing away unexpectedly about six months later. That piece of advice will forever remain some of the most valuable words ever spoken to me. It ended up being so very true.

A few months later, we began the adoption process. After a very hard and frustrating adoption process, God led us to our new son. Had we become pregnant through IVF, we would have missed him. Who knows how we would have ended up being his parents, if ever. He was born to be our ours, and he indeed needed us sooner than I could have ever imagined. He was a very sick, very malnourished little boy who needed us as much as we needed him. He was abandoned, left to die in the jungle, sitting in a small circular basin, and by chance was found by a cattle herder. After being hospitalized, with no one to claim him, he was put in an orphanage and given the name as my husband's name. See God's plan here? It's amazing!

That little boy was born to be our son. And we were meant to be his parents. Had we stuck with trying IVF again and again, we would have missed him, missed out on being his parents, missed out on all God had planned for us to be a family. Our two sons are the best brothers in the world. They love and protect each other, and I couldn't imagine life without either one of them. God is redeeming.

Megan's Story

In one way, redemption for me will be one day smothering Eliana in kisses and hugs. But in another way, I experience redemption by talking about her and sharing my story with other grieving mommas. I allowed God to transform a sad, depressing story into a beautiful one. Before I lost Eliana, I would have been nervous to talk to anyone about losing their baby. But now, instead of shying away, I am able to go to them boldly knowing God places people in our lives for such a purpose.

Losing Eliana brought me closer to Jesus. Her life and struggle to survive brought faith back into my life. Even though the odds were against her for those few weeks, she was alive in me, I fought for her, and I prayed for her with all my might. I was blessed beyond words by the women who reached out to me. Even when one woman was going through her own recent loss, pain, and hurt, she blessed me and helped me to heal. I wouldn't have accepted and processed my loss without that community surrounding me. And I know that God had his hand on all of it.

One thing that I want every grieving woman to know is this: your baby is a real person. No matter how early you lost your precious one, don't let doctors, strangers, friends, or family make you feel any different. Your baby may only have had a tiny little heart, but that small heartbeat has a big purpose in heaven and on earth. If you are open to it, this can be your ministry too. It's painful no matter the details of your loss. Allow God to heal the pain, and he will open up doors for healing. That is his promise.

God's Promise

The Spirit of the Sovereign LORD is on me,
because the LORD has anointed me
to proclaim good news to the poor.
He has sent me to bind up the brokenhearted,
to proclaim freedom for the captives
and release from darkness for the prisoners,
to proclaim the year of the LORD's favor

and the day of vengeance of our God,
to comfort all who mourn,
and provide for those who grieve in Zion—
to bestow on them a crown of beauty
instead of ashes,
the oil of joy
instead of mourning,
and a garment of praise
instead of a spirit of despair.
They will be called oaks of righteousness,
a planting of the LORD
for the display of his splendor.

Isaiah 61:1–3 (NIV)

A Prayer

My redeeming Savior,

As I remember the life of my baby, I am also reminded of how steadfast your love and tender your care were for me during the darkest of nights. My baby's life continues to blossom love and reveal your truth inside of me. Thank you for my baby's life, and thank you for the mark that has been made on my heart. May that mark always testify to your unconditional love, unchanging goodness and unwavering faithfulness. May my baby's life give a glimpse of your light to a hurting world. May I walk alongside other mommas who are broken by the losses of babies. May both my grief and my healing be used for the glory of your name. Thank you that I can have confidence knowing none of my pain is wasted when I place details of my loss in your hands. You are a God that redeems. In Jesus's precious name, amen.

Journal

The loss of a baby has a way of sifting out the things in our lives that don't matter. Our priorities shift, our perspective changes, and the very way that we live becomes more intentional. Walking through the painful, arid desert of losing a baby transforms the way we view the world. We are keenly aware of the tiniest forms of beauty that otherwise would have been overlooked. We experience the supernatural comfort and healing of Jesus that we would not have ever known without our baby's life. We learn who God has created us to be in a deeper and more detailed way. The glimpses of truth and beauty that we see during our journeys of grief do not void our loss or pain, but they give evidence of the healing towards which we are traveling. God's redemption of our brokenness transforms a circumstance that on its own would remain hopeless and despairing, into a story of strength and healing and hope of eternity!

What mark of redemption does your life now bear? How have you seen God use your loss, grief, or pain to flourish into something good, even joy-filled, in your life and the lives of others? What truths about God can you carry into all future seasons of your life?

About the Author

Heather Butler is a proud Colorado native, currently living in the Rocky Mountains with her lumberjack-esque husband and their three small humans. She is also the momma of two precious babies on that side of heaven—Lavender and Pine. While rocking her daughter to sleep one night, the idea of a book was breathed into her heart and she felt the Lord whisper, "Tell others about my faithfulness." She is passionate about walking alongside other women who are grieving the loss of a baby.

When Heather is not chasing toddlers or cleaning up crushed graham crackers off the floor, she loves going on adrenaline-fueled adventures with her husband. She is also obsessed with roaming the mountains and feeling God's heartbeat in the massiveness of nature.

She writes about life, loss, hope, and God's faithfulness on her personal blog, **FaithfulnessDeclared.com**. She is also a monthly contributor for Pregnancy After Loss Support, an online magazine that offers valuable resources, support, and encouragement to women who are pregnant after experiencing a previous loss.